D0112755

BEYOND VIOLENCE

J. KRISHNAMURTI

BEYOND VIOLENCE

Harper & Row, Publishers
NEW YORK, EVANSTON, SAN FRANCISCO, LONDON

UNITY SCHOOL LIBRARY
UNITY VILLAGE, MISSOURI 64065

BEYOND VIOLENCE: Copyright © 1973 by Krishnamurti Foundation Trust Ltd., London. For information address Krishnamurti Foundation of America, P.O. Box 216, Ojai, California 93023.
All rights reserved. Printed in the United States of America. No part of this book may be used or reproduced in any manner whatsoever without written permission except in the case of brief quotations embodied in critical articles and reviews. For information address Harper & Row, Publishers, Inc., 10 East 53rd Street, New York, N.Y. 10022. Published simultaneously in Canada by Fitzhenry & Whiteside Limited, Toronto.

STANDARD BOOK NUMBER: 06-064839-2

LIBRARY OF CONGRESS CATALOG CARD NUMBER: 72-9875

'We have built a society which is violent and we, as
human beings, are violent; the environment, the culture
in which we live, is the product of our endeavour, of
our struggle, of our pain, of our appalling brutalities.
So the most important question is: is it possible to end
this tremendous violence in oneself?'

'We are violent. Throughout existence, human
beings have been violent and are violent. I want to find
out, as a human being, how to transcend this violence,
how to go beyond it. What am I to do? I see what violence has done in the world, how it has destroyed every
form of relationship, how it has brought deep agony in
oneself, misery—I see all that. And I say to myself, I
want to live a really peaceful life in which there is a deep
abundance of love—all the violence must go. Now what
have I to do?'

CONTENTS

TALKS AND DISCUSSIONS

Part I

Part II

PART I

I

EXISTENCE

'Technologically, man has advanced incredibly, yet he remains as he has been for thousands of years, fighting, greedy, envious, burdened with great sorrow.'

I WOULD LIKE to talk about the whole problem of existence. Probably you know as well as the speaker what is actually taking place in the world—utter chaos, disorder, violence, extreme forms of brutality, riots ending up in war. Our lives are extraordinarily difficult, confused and contradictory, not only in ourselves—inside the skin as it were—but also outwardly. There is utter destruction. All the values are changing from day to day, there is no respect, no authority, and nobody has faith in anything whatsoever; neither in the Church, nor in the establishment, nor in any philosophy. So one is left absolutely to oneself to find out what one is to do in this chaotic world. What is the right action?—if there is such a thing as right action.

I am sure each one of us asks what is the right conduct. This is a very serious question, and I hope those of you who are here are really serious, because this is not a gathering for philosophical or religious entertainment. We are not indulging in any theory, in any philosophy, or bringing from the East some exotic ideas. What we are going to do together, is to examine the facts as they are, very closely, objectively, non-sentimentally, unemotionally. And to explore in that way, there must be freedom from prejudice, freedom from any conditioning, from any philosophy, from any belief; we are going to explore together very slowly, patiently, hesitantly, to find out. It is like good scientists looking through a microscope and seeing exactly the same thing. Because if you are a scientist in the laboratory using a microscope, you must show what you see to another scientist, so that both of you see exactly what is. And that is what we are going to do. There is not your microscope, or the speaker's : there is only one precision-instrument through which we are going to observe and learn in the observation—not learn according to your temperament, your conditioning, or to your particular form of belief, but merely observe what actually is, and thereby learn. And in the learning is the doing—learning is not separate from action.

So what we are going to do first, is to understand what it means to communicate. Inevitably we have to use words, but it is much more important to go beyond the words. Which means that you and the speaker are going to take a journey of investigation together, where each one of us is in constant communion with the other; that is sharing together, exploring together, observing together. For that word communication means partaking, sharing. Therefore there is no teacher or disciple, there is not the speaker to whom you listen, either agreeing or disagreeing—which would be absurd. If we are communicating, then there is no question of agreement or disagreement, because both of us are looking, both of us are examining, not from your point of view, or from the speaker's point of view.

That is why it is very important to find out how to observe, how to look with clear eyes, how to listen so that there is no distortion. It is your responsibility as well as the speaker's to share together—we are going to work together. This must be very clearly understood from the beginning : we are not indulging in any form of sentimentality or emotionalism.

If this is clear, that you and the speaker, being free from our prejudices, from our beliefs, from our particular conditioning and knowledge, are free to examine, then we can proceed; bearing in mind that we are using a precision-instrument—the microscope—and that you and the speaker must see the same thing; otherwise it will not be possible to communicate. As this is a very serious matter, you must not only be free to examine it but free to apply it, free to test it out in daily life; not keep it merely as a theory or as a principle towards which you are working.

Now let us look at what is actually going on in the world; there is violence of every kind, not only outwardly but also in our relationship with each other. There are infinite nationalistic and religious divisions between people, each against the other, both politically and individually. Seeing this vast confusion, this immense sorrow, what are you to do? Can you look to anybody to tell you what to do?—to the priest, to the specialist, to the analyst? They have not brought about peace or happiness, joy, freedom to live. So where are you to look? If you assume the responsibility of your own authority as an individual, because you no longer have any faith in outward authority—we are using the word 'authority' advisedly in a particular sense of that word—then you as an individual, will you look for your own authority inwardly?

The word 'individuality' means 'indivisible', not fragmented. Individuality means a totality, the whole, and the word 'whole' means healthy, holy. But you are not an individual, you are not sane, because you are broken up, fragmented in yourself; you are in contradiction with yourself, separated, therefore you are not an individual at all. So out of this fragmentation how can you ask that one fragment assume authority over the other fragments?

Please do see this very clearly, this is what we are examining; because we see that education, science, organised religion, propaganda, politics, have failed. They have not brought about peace, though technologically man has advanced incredibly. Yet man remains as he has been for thousands of years, fighting, greedy, envious, violent, and burdened with great sorrow. That is the fact; that is not an assumption.

So to find out what to do in a world that is so confused, so brutal, so utterly unhappy, we have to examine not only what living is—actually as it is—but also we have to understand what love is; and what it means to die. Also we have to understand what man has been trying to find out for thousands of years : if there is a reality which transcends all thought. Until you understand the complexity of this whole picture, to say, 'What am I to do with regard to a particular fragment?' has no meaning whatsoever. You have to understand the whole of existence, not just a part of it; however tiresome, however agonising, however brutal that part is, you have to see the whole picture—the picture of what love is, what meditation is, if there is such a thing as God, what it means to live. We have to understand this phenomenon of existence as a whole. Only then can you ask the question, 'What am I to do?' And if you see this whole picture, probably you will never ask that question—then you will be living and then the living is the right action.

So first we are going to see what is living, and what is not living. We have to understand what that word 'to observe' means. To see, to hear and to learn—what does it mean 'to see'?

When we are together looking at something, it doesn't mean 'togetherness'. It means that you and the speaker are going to look. What does that word 'to look' mean? It is quite a difficult thing to look; one has to have the art. Probably you have never looked at a tree; because when you do look, all your botanical knowledge comes in and prevents you from observing it actually as it is. Probably you have never looked at your wife or your husband or your boy-friend or girl-friend, because you have an image about her or him. The image that you have built about her or him, or about yourself, is going to prevent you from looking. Therefore when you look there is distortion, there is contradiction. So when you look there must be a relationship between the observer and the thing observed. Please do listen to this because it needs great care. You know, when you care for something you do observe very closely; which means you have great affection; then you are capable of observing.

So looking together means to observe with care, with affection, so that we see the same thing together. But first, there must be freedom from the image that you have about yourself. Please, do it as it is being said; the speaker is merely a mirror and therefore what you see is yourself in the mirror. So the speaker is in no way important; what is important is what you see in that mirror. And to see clearly, precisely, without any distortion, every form of image must go—the image that you are an American or a Catholic, that you are a rich man or a poor man, all your prejudices must go. And all that goes the moment you see clearly what is in front of you, because what you see is much more important than what you 'should do' from what you see. The moment you see very clearly, there is action from that clarity. It is only the mind that is chaotic, confused, choosing, that says, 'What am I to do?' There is the danger of nationalism, the division between peoples; that division is the greatest danger because in division there is insecurity, there is war, there is uncertainty. But when the mind sees the danger of division very clearly—not intellectually, not emotionally, but actually sees it—then there is a totally different kind of action.

So it is very important to learn to see, to observe. And what is it we are observing? Not the outer phenomenon only, but the inward state of man. Because unless there is a fundamental, radical revolution in the psyche, in the very root of one's being, mere trimming, mere legislation on the periphery, has very little meaning. So what we are concerned with is whether man, as he is, can radically bring about a trans-formation in himself; not according to a particular theory, a particular philosophy, but by seeing actually what he is. That very perception of what he is, will bring about the radical change. And to see what he is, is of the highest importance—not what he thinks he is, not what he is told that he is.

There is a difference between when you are told that you are hungry and actually being hungry. The two states are entirely different; in one you know actually through your own direct perception and feeling that you are hungry, then you act. But if you are told by somebody that you might be hungry, quite a different activity takes place. So similarly, one has to observe and see for oneself actually what one is. And that is what we are going to do : know oneself. It has been stated that to know oneself is the highest wisdom, but very few of us have done it. We have not the patience, the intensity or the passion, to find out what we are. We have the energy, but we have given that energy over to others; we have to be told what we are.

We are going to find this out by observing ourselves, because the moment there is a radical change in what we are, we shall bring about peace in the world. We shall live freely—not do what we like, but live happily, joyously. A man who has great joy in his heart has no hatred, no violence, he will not bring about the destruction of another. Freedom means no condemnation whatsoever of what you see in yourself. Most of us condemn, or explain away or justify—we never look without justification or condemnation. Therefore the first thing to do—and probably it's the last thing to do—is to observe without any form of condemnation. This is going to be very difficult, because all our culture, our tradition, is to compare, justify or condemn what we are. We say 'this is right', 'this is wrong', 'this is true', 'this is false', 'this is beautiful', which prevents us from actually observing what we are.

Please listen to this : what you are is a living thing, and when you condemn what you see in yourself, you are condemning it with a memory which is dead, which is the past. Therefore there is a contradiction between the living and the past. To understand the living, the past must go, so that you can look. You are doing this now, as we are talking; you are not going back home to think about it. Because the moment you think about it you are already finished. This is not group-therapy, not a public confession—which is immature. What we are doing is to explore into ourselves like scientists, not depending on anybody. If you trust anybody you are lost, whether you trust your analyst, your priest, or your own memory, your own experience; because that is the past. And if you are looking with the eyes of the past at the present, then you will never understand what the living thing is.

So we are examining together this living thing, which is you, life, whatever that is; that means we are looking at this phenomenon of violence, first at the violence in ourselves and then at the outward violence. When we have understood the violence in ourselves then it may not be necessary to look at the outward violence, because what we are inwardly, we project outwardly. By nature, through heredity, through so-called evolution, we have brought about this violence in ourselves. That is a fact: we are violent human beings. There are a thousand explanations why we are violent. We will not indulge in explanations, because we can get lost, with each specialist saying, 'This is the cause of violence'. The more explanations we have, the more we think we understand, but the thing remains as it is. So please bear in mind all the time that the description is not the described; what is explained is not what is. There are many explanations which are fairly simple and obvious—overcrowded cities, over-population, heredity and all the rest of it; we can brush all that aside. The fact remains that we are violent people. From childhood we are brought up to be violent, competitive, beastly to one another. We have never faced the fact. What we have said is : 'What shall we do about violence?'

Please do listen to this with care, that is with affection, with attention. The moment you put that question : 'What shall we do about it?' your answer will always be according to the past. Because that is the only thing you know : your whole existence is based on the past, your life *is* the past. If you have ever looked at yourself properly, you will see to what an extraordinary extent you are living in the past. All thinking—into which we shall go presently—is the response of the past, the response of memory, knowledge and experience. So thinking is never new, never free. With this process of thinking you look at life, and therefore when you ask, 'What shall I do about violence?' you have already escaped from the fact.

So can we learn, observe, what violence is? Now, how do you look at it? Do you condemn it? Do you justify it? If you do not, then how do you look at it? Please do this as we are talking about it—it is tremendously important. Do you look at this phenomenon, which is yourself as a violent human being, as an outsider looking within? Or do you look at it without the outsider, without the censor? When you look, do you look as an observer, different from the thing you look at—as one who says, 'I am not violent, but I want to get rid of violence'? When you look that way you are assuming one fragment to be more important than the other fragments.

When you look as one fragment looking at the other fragments, then that one fragment has assumed authority, and that fragment causes contradiction and therefore conflict. But if you can look without any fragment, then you look at the whole without the observer. Are you following all this? So sir, *do* it! Because then you will see an extraordinary thing taking place, then you will have no conflict whatsoever. Conflict is what we are, what we live with. At home, in the office, when you are asleep, all the time, we are in conflict, there is constant battle and contradiction.

So until you understand the root of this contradiction yourself—not according to the speaker, not according to anybody—you can have no life of peace and happiness and joy. Therefore it is essential that you understand what causes conflict and therefore contradiction, what the root of it is. The root is this division between the observer and the thing observed. The observer says, 'I must get rid of violence', or 'I am living a life of non-violence' when he *is* violent—which is a pretence, hypocrisy. So to find out what causes this division is of the highest importance.

You are listening to a speaker who has no authority, who is not your teacher, because there is no guru, there is no follower; there are only human beings, trying to discover a life without conflict, to live peacefully, to live with a great abundance of love. But if you follow anybody you are destroying yourself and the other. (*Applause.*) Please do not clap. I am not trying to entertain you, I am not looking for your applause. What is important is that you and I understand, and live a different kind of life—not this stupid life that one leads. And your applause, your agreement or disagreement does not change that fact.

It is very important to understand for oneself, to see, through one's own observation, that conflict must exist everlastingly as long as there is a division between the observer and the observed. And in you there is this division, as the 'I', as the 'self', as the 'me' that is trying to be different from somebody else. Is this clear? Clarity means that you see it for yourself. This is not just a verbal clarity, hearing a set of words or ideas; it means that you yourself see very clearly, and therefore without choice, how this division between the observer and the observed creates mischief, confusion and sorrow. So when you are violent, can you look at that violence in yourself without the memory, the justification, the assertion that you must not be violent—but merely look? Which means that you must be free of the past. To look means that you must have great energy, you must have intensity. You must have passion, otherwise you cannot look. Unless you have great passion and intensity you cannot look at the beauty of a cloud, or the marvellous hills that you have here. In the same way, to look at oneself without the observer needs tremendous energy and passion. And this passion, this intensity, is destroyed when you begin to condemn, to justify, when you say, 'I must not', 'I must', or when you say, 'I am living a non-violent life', or pretend to live a non-violent life.

That is why all ideologies are most destructive. In India they have talked about non-violence from time immemorial. They have said, 'We are practising non-violence' and they are just as violent as anybody else. The ideal gives them a certain sense of hypocritical escape from the fact. If you can put aside all ideologies, all principles and just face the fact, then you are dealing with something actual, not mythical, not theoretical.

So that is the first thing : to observe without the observer; to look at your wife, at your children, without the image. The image may be a superficial image or deeply hidden in the unconscious; one has not only to observe the image that one has put together outwardly, but also the images that one has deep down inwardly—the image of the race, of the culture, the historical perspective of the image that one has about oneself. So one must observe not only at the conscious level, but also at the hidden level, in the deep recesses of one's own mind.

I do not know if you have ever observed the unconscious. Are you interested in all this? Do you know how difficult all this is? It is very easy to quote somebody, or to repeat what your analyst, or the professor has told you; that is child's play. But if you do not merely read books about these things, then it becomes extraordinarily arduous. It is part of your meditation to find out how to look at the unconscious; not through dreams, not through intuition, because your intuition may be your wish, your desire, your hidden hope. So you have to find out how to look at the image that you have created about yourself outwardly—the symbol—and also to look deeply within yourself.

One must be aware not only of outward things, but also of the inward movement of life, the inward movement of desires, motives, anxieties, fears, sorrows. Now, to be aware without choice is to be aware of the colour that somebody is wearing, without saying, 'I like it' or, 'I don't like it', but just to observe; as you sit in a bus, to observe the movement of your own thought without condemning, without justifying, without choosing. When you so look you will see there is no 'observer'. The observer is the 'censor', the American, the Catholic, the Protestant; he is the result of propaganda; he is the past. And when the past looks, it must inevitably separate, condemn or justify. A man who is hungry, who is really in sorrow, does he say, 'If I do this, will I get that?' He wants to be rid of sorrow or he wants to fill his stomach; he never talks about theories. So sir, first, if I may suggest, rid yourself of the idea of 'if'. Do not live somewhere in the future; the future is what you project *now*. The now is the past; that is what you are when you say, 'I am living now'. You are living in the past, because the past is directing and shaping you; memories of the past are making you act this way or that way.

So 'to live' is to be free of time; and when you say 'if', you are introducing time. And time is the greatest sorrow.

Questioner: How can we be ourselves to each other?

KRISHNAMURTI: Listen to that question: 'to be ourselves'. What is 'yourself' may I ask? When you say 'ourselves to another', what is yourself? Your anger, your bitterness, your frustrations, your despairs, your violence, your hopes, your utter lack of love—is that what you are? No, sir, do not say, 'How can I be myself with another?'—you don't know yourself. You are all this, and the other is also all that—his misery, his problems, his moods, his frustrations, his ambitions; each lives in isolation, in exclusion. It is only when these barriers, these resistances, disappear that you can live with another happily.

Questioner: Why do you separate the conscious from the unconscious when you do not believe in separation?

KRISHNAMURTI : That is what *you* do—I don't! (*Laughter.*) You have been taught, during the last few decades, that you have an unconscious, and volumes have been written about it; the analysts are making fortunes out of it. Water remains water : whether you put it in a golden jug or in an earthenware pot, it is water. In the same way, not to divide but to see the whole : that is our problem, to see the whole of consciousness, not a particular fragment as the conscious or the unconscious. To see the whole of it is one of the most difficult things to do, but to see a fragment is fairly easy. To see something whole, which means to see it sanely, healthily, wholly, you must have no centre from which you look—the centre as 'the me', as 'the you', as 'the they', as 'the we'.

This is not a discourse, this is not a talk or a lecture to which you listen casually and go away. You are listening to yourself; if you have the ears to hear what is being said you cannot agree or disagree—it is there. Therefore we are sharing it together, we are communicating, we are working together. In that there is great freedom, great affection, compassion, and after all, out of *that* comes understanding.

Santa Monica, California. 1 March 1970.

2

FREEDOM

'Unless the mind is absolutely free from fear, every form of action brings about more mischief, more misery, more confusion.'

W E   W E R E   S A Y I N G how important it is that there should be a fundamental change in the human psyche and that this change can only come about through complete freedom. That word 'freedom' is a most dangerous word unless we understand completely and absolutely what it means; we have to learn the full implications of that word, not just its meaning according to the dictionary. Most of us use it according to our particular tendency, or fancy, or politically. We are going to use that word neither politically nor circumstantially, but rather go into the inward, psychological meaning of it.

But before that, we have to understand the meaning of the word 'learn'. As we said the other day, we are going to communicate together—which means partake, share together—and learning is part of this. You are not going to learn from the speaker, but you learn by observing, by using the speaker as a mirror to observe your own movement of thought, of feeling, your own psyche, your own psychology. There is no authority involved in this at all; though the speaker has to sit on a platform, because it is convenient, that position does not give him any authority whatsoever. So we can brush that aside completely and consider the question of learning—not from another, but using the speaker to learn about oneself. You are learning from observing your own psyche, your own self—whatever it is. To learn, there must be freedom, there must be a great deal of curiosity and there must be intensity, passion, an immediacy. You cannot learn if there is no passion, no energy to find out. If there is any kind of prejudice, any bias, of like or dislike, of condemnation, then one cannot possibly learn, one only distorts what one observes.

The word 'discipline' means to learn from a man who knows; you are supposed not to know, so you learn from another. The word 'discipline' implies that. But here we are using the word 'discipline' not as learning from another, but as the observing of oneself, which demands a discipline which is not suppression, imitation or conformity, or even adjustment, but actually observing; that very observation is an act of discipline—which is learning through observation. That very act of learning is its own discipline, in the sense that you have to give a great deal of attention, you have to have great energy, intensity, and the immediacy of action.

We are going to talk about fear, and in going into that we have to consider a great many things, because fear is a very complex problem. Unless the mind is absolutely free from fear, every form of action brings about more mischief, more misery, more confusion. So we are going to enquire together into the implication of fear and whether it is at all possible to be completely free of it—not tomorrow, not at some future date, but so that as you leave this hall, the burden, the darkness, the misery and the corruption of fear no longer exists.

To understand this you have to examine also the idea that we have of gradualness—that is, the idea of gradually getting rid of fear. There is no such thing as gradually getting rid of fear. Either you are completely free of it, or not at all; there is no gradualness, which implies time—time not only in the chronological sense of that word, but also in the psychological sense. Time is of the very essence of fear, as we shall point out presently. So in understanding and being free of fear and the conditioning in which one is brought up, the idea of doing it slowly, eventually, must completely come to an end. That is going to be our first difficulty.

If I may point out again, this is not a lecture; it is rather that two friendly, affectionate people, enquire together into a very difficult problem. Man has lived with fear, he has accepted it as part of his life and we are enquiring into the possibility, or rather the 'impossibility', of ending fear. You know, what is possible is already done, is already finished—is it not? If it is possible you can do it. But what is impossible becomes possible only when you understand that there is no tomorrow at all—psychologically speaking. We are confronted with the extraordinary problem of fear, and man apparently has never been able to be rid of it completely. Not only physically, but inwardly, psychologically, he has never been rid of it; he has always escaped from it through various forms of entertainment, religious and otherwise. And the escapes have been an avoidance of 'what is'. So we are concerned with the 'impossibility' of being free from it completely —therefore what is 'impossible' becomes possible.

What actually is fear? The physical fears can be understood comparatively easily. But the psychological fears are much more complex, and to understand them there must be freedom to enquire—not to form an opinion, not a dialectical enquiry into the possibility of ending fear. But first let us go into the question of physical fears, which naturally affect the psyche. When you meet danger of any kind there is instant physical response. Is that fear?

(You are not learning from me, we are learning together; therefore you have to pay a great deal of attention, because it is no good coming to a gathering of this kind and going away with a few sets of ideas, or formulas—that doesn't free the mind from fear. But what does free the mind from fear completely and absolutely, is to understand it totally *now*—not tomorrow. It is like seeing something wholly, completely; and what you see you understand. Then it is yours and nobody else's.)

So there is physical fear, like seeing a precipice, meeting a wild animal. Is the response to meeting such a danger, physical fear, or is it intelligence? You meet a snake, and you respond immediately. That response is the past conditioning which says 'be careful' and your whole psychosomatic response is immediate, though conditioned; it is the result of the past, for you were told that the animal is dangerous. In meeting any form of physical danger, is there fear? Or is it the response of intelligence to the necessity of self-preservation?

Then there is the fear of having again a previous physical pain or illness. What takes place there? Is that intelligence? Or is it an action of thought, which is the response of memory, fearing that the pain which one had in the past might happen again? Is this clear, that thought produces fear? There are also the various forms of psychological fears—fear of death, fear of society, fear of not being respectable, fear of what people might say, fear of darkness and so on.

Before we go into this question of psychological fears, we have to understand something very clearly: we are not analysing. Analysis has nothing whatsoever to do with observation, with seeing. In analysis there is always the analyser and the thing analysed. The analyser is a fragment of the many other fragments of which we are compounded. One fragment assumes the authority of the analyser and begins to analyse. Now, what is involved in that? The analyser is the censor, the entity who assumes that he has knowledge and therefore he has the authority to analyse. Unless he analyses completely, truly, without any distortion, his analysis has no value at all. Please do understand this very clearly, because the speaker does not maintain the necessity of any analysis whatsoever, at any time. It is rather a bitter pill to swallow, because most of you either have been analysed, or are going to be analysed, or have studied what analysis is. Analysis implies not only an analyser separate from the analysed, but it also implies time. You have to analyse gradually, bit by bit, the whole series of fragments of which you are, and that takes years. And when you analyse, the mind must be absolutely clear and free.

So several things are involved : the analyser, a fragment who separates himself from other fragments and says, 'I am going to analyse', and also time, day after day, looking, criticising, condemning, judging, evaluating, remembering. Also implied is the whole drama of dreams; one never asks if it is necessary to dream at all—though all the psychologists say you must, otherwise you will go mad.

So who is the analyser? He is part of yourself, part of your mind, and he is going to examine the other parts; he is the result of past experiences, past knowledge, past evaluation; he is the centre from which he is going to examine. Has that centre any truth, any validity? All of us function from a centre and what is that centre? That centre is a centre of fear, anxiety, greed, pleasure, despair, hope, dependency, ambition, comparison—it is that from which we think and act. This is not a supposition, not a theory, but an absolute, observable, daily fact. In that centre there are many fragments and one of the fragments becomes the analyser—which is absurd, because the analyser is the analysed. You must understand this, otherwise you will not be able to follow when we go into the question of fear much more deeply. You have to understand it completely, because when you leave this hall you must be free of it so that you can live, enjoy and look at the world with different eyes; so that you can have your relationships no longer burdened with fear, with jealousy, with despair; so that you become a human being, not a violent, destructive animal.

So the analyser is the analysed, and in the separation between the analyser and the analysed is the whole process of conflict. And analysis involves time : by the time you have analysed everything, you are ready for the grave and you have not lived at all. (*Laughter.*) No, do not laugh; this is not an entertainment, this is dreadfully serious. It is only the earnest, serious person who knows what life is, what living is —not the man who seeks amusement. Therefore this demands a great deal of earnest inquiry.

The mind must be completely free of the idea of analysis, because it has no meaning. You must see this not because the speaker says so, but by seeing the truth of the whole process of analysis. And the truth will bring understanding; truth *is* understanding—of the falseness of analysis. Therefore when you see what is false, you can put it aside completely. It is only when we do not see, that we are confused.

Now can we look into fear as a whole—not into the multitudinous psychological fears, but into fear?—there is only one fear. Though there may be different causes of fear, brought about through various reactions and influences, there is only fear. And fear does not exist by itself, it exists in relation to something, which is fairly simple and obvious. One is afraid of something—of the future, of the past, of not being able to fulfil, afraid of not being loved, of living a lonely, miserable life, of old age and death.

So there is fear, both recognisable and hidden. What we are enquiring into is not any particular form of fear but the totality of it, the conscious as well as the hidden. How does it happen? In asking that question you also have to ask: what is pleasure? Because fear and pleasure go together. You cannot discard fear without understanding pleasure; they are the two sides of one coin. So in understanding the truth about fear, you also understand the truth about pleasure. To want only pleasure and have no fear, is an impossible demand. Whereas if you understood both, you would have quite a different appreciation, a different understanding of them. Which means that we have to learn about the structure and the nature of fear as well as of pleasure. You cannot be free of one and hold on to the other.

So what is fear and what is pleasure? As you can observe in yourself, you want to get rid of fear. All life is an escape from fear. Your gods, your churches, your moralities are based on fear, and to understand that you have to understand how this fear comes about. You have done something in the past and you do not want another to find out; that is one form of fear. You are afraid of the future because you have no job, or you are frightened of something else. So you are afraid of the past, and you are afraid of the future. Fear comes when thought looks back to things that have happened in the past, or to events that may happen in the future. *Thought is responsible for this.* You have very carefully avoided—especially in America—thinking about death; but it is always there. You do not want to think about it, because the moment you do, you are afraid. And because you are afraid, you have theories about it; you believe in resurrection, in re-incarnation—you have dozens of beliefs—all because you are afraid and all of which arise from thought. Thought creates and sustains the fear of yesterday and of tomorrow, and thought also sustains pleasure. You have seen a beautiful sunset; at that moment there is great joy, the beauty of the light on the water and the movement of the trees; there is great delight. Then thought comes along and says, 'How I wish I could have it again'. You begin to think about it and you go to that place again tomorrow and you do not see it. You have sexual pleasure and you think about it, you chew on it, you build images, pictures; and thought sustains that. There is thought sustaining pleasure and thought sustaining fear. So thought is responsible. This is not a formula for you to learn, but an actuality to understand together; therefore there is no agreement or disagreement.

So, what is thought? Thought is obviously the response of memory. If you had no memory there would be no thought. If you had no memory of the road to your house, you would not get home. So thought not only breeds and sustains fear and pleasure, but thought is also necessary to function, to act, efficiently. See how difficult it becomes: thought must be employed completely, objectively, when you function technologically, when you do anything, and thought also breeds fear and pleasure and therefore pain.

So one asks oneself the question: what place has thought? Where is the border-line between where thought must be employed completely and where it must not interfere—as when you see the most beautiful sunset and live it at the moment and forget it at that moment. The whole process of thinking is never free because it has its roots in the past; thought is never new. There is no question of freedom in choice because thought is in operation when you choose. So we have a very subtle problem, which is : one sees the danger of thought which brings about fear—fear destroys, perverts, makes the mind live in darkness, in misery—yet one sees that thought must be used efficiently, objectively, without emotion. What is the state of your mind—as you observe this fact?

Look, sirs, it is most important to understand this very clearly, because it is no good your sitting there listening to a lot of words that have no meaning, when at the end of it, you are still afraid. When you leave there must be no fear, not because you hypnotise yourself that there is no fear, but because you have understood actually, psychologically, inwardly, the whole structure of fear.

That is why it is very important to learn, to look. What we are doing is to observe very closely how fear comes into being. When you think about death, or about losing your job, when you think about a dozen things, either of the past or of the future, there is the inevitability of fear. When the mind sees the fact that thought must function and also sees the danger of thought, what is the quality of the mind that is seeing this? You have to find out, not wait for me to tell you.

Please listen carefully; it is so simple, really. We said analysis is no good, and we explained why. If you saw the truth of it you have understood it. Before, you accepted analysis, as part of your conditioning. Now, when you see the futility, the falseness of analysis, it has dropped away. So what is the state of the mind that has put aside analysis? It is freer, is it not? Therefore it is more alive, more active and therefore much more intelligent, sharper, more sensitive. And when you have seen the fact, as to how fear comes into being, have learnt about it and watched also the process of pleasure, then watch your state of mind, which is becoming much more acute, much clearer, therefore tremendously intelligent. This intelligence has nothing whatsoever to do with knowledge, with experience; you cannot arrive at this intelligence by going to college and learning how to be sensitive. This intelligence comes when you have observed very closely the whole structure of analysis and what is implied in it—the time involved and the stupidity of thinking that one fragment is going to clear up the whole process—and when you have seen the nature of fear and understood what pleasure is.

So when fear—which has become a habit—comes upon you tomorrow, you will know how to meet it and not postpone it. And the very meeting of it is the ending of it at that moment, because intelligence is in operation. That means ending not only the known fears, but also the deep, hidden fears.

You know, one of the most strange things is the ease with which we are influenced. From childhood we are brought up to be Catholic, Protestant, American, or whatever it is. We are the result of repeated propaganda and we keep on repeating it. We are second-hand human beings. Therefore be on your guard not to be influenced by the speaker, because you are dealing with your life, not his life.

Going into the question of pleasure, one also has to understand what real enjoyment is, for it has nothing to do with pleasure. Has pleasure, desire, anything to do with love? To understand all this one has to observe oneself. One is the result of the world; one is a human being who is part of the other human beings, who all have the same problems, perhaps not economic or social, but human problems—all fighting, making tremendous efforts and saying to themselves that life has no meaning whatsoever as it is lived. So one invents formulas for living. All that becomes utterly unnecessary when you understand the structure of yourself, and of fear, pleasure, love, and the meaning of death. Then only can you live as a total human being and never do anything wrong.

So, if you want to, ask questions, bearing in mind that the question and the answer is within yourself.

Questioner: If fear is generated by an unknown and you say that using thought is a wrong way of going about understanding it . . .?

KRISHNAMURTI : You say you are frightened of the unknown, either of the unknown of tomorrow, or of the real unknown. Is it that you are frightened of something you do not know? Or are you frightened of something you do know, to which you are attached? Therefore are you frightened of leaving the known? Have you understood, sir? When you are frightened of death, are you frightened of the unknown? Or are you frightened of all the things you have known coming to an end, your pleasures, your family, your achievements, your success, your furniture? How can one be frightened of something one does not know? And if you are frightened of it, thought wants to take it into the field of the known, therefore it begins to imagine. Therefore your God is the product of your imagination or your fear. Sir, therefore do not speculate about the unknown. Understand the known and be free of the known.

Questioner: I have read the expression 'Father, I believe, help my disbelief'. How can we accomplish anything with this apparent conflict of belief and doubt?

KRISHNAMURTI : Why do you believe anything that you read? It does not matter whether it is in the Bible or in the Gita or in the sacred books of other religions. Do look at it— why do you believe? Do you believe in the sunrise tomorrow?

You believe in a sense—you think it will arise. But you believe in heaven, you believe in a Father, you believe in something—why? Because you are afraid, you are unhappy, lonely, because of fear of death, you believe in something that you think is permanent. How can a mind that is burdened with beliefs see clearly? How can it be free to observe? How can such a mind love? You have your belief and another has his belief. In understanding the whole problem of fear, one has no belief whatsoever. The mind then functions happily, without distortion and therefore there is great joy, ecstasy.

Questioner: I have read your books and I listen to you speak and I hear you say beautiful things. I hear you speak of fear and how we should eliminate it; but the nature of the mind is to be full of desire, to be full of thoughts. How are we to experience freedom of mind as long as the mind is constantly active? What is the system?

KRISHNAMURTI: Sir, what is desire? Why does the mind chatter so endlessly?

Questioner: Dissatisfaction.

KRISHNAMURTI: Please do not answer, find out. Look: you want a system, a method, a discipline to quieten the mind, to understand this or that or to put aside desire. The practising of a system means a mechanical routine, doing the same thing over and over again; that is what a system implies. What takes place when the mind does that? It becomes a dull, stupid mind. One has to understand why the mind chatters, why the mind goes from one thing to another.

I do not think I can go into it this evening—are you not tired? (*Cries of 'no'.*) You have had a long day in the office;

there it was routine. Here you say you are not tired, which means you have not been working. (*Laughter.*) You have not been sustaining serious investigation. That means you are just being entertained and will go away with your fears. And for God's sake, sirs, what is the point of it?

Santa Monica, California. 4 March 1970.

3

INWARD REVOLUTION

'Change in society is of secondary importance; that will come about naturally, inevitably, when you as a human being bring about this change in yourself.'

W E W E R E C O N S I D E R I N G the extraordinary complexity of everyday life, the strife, the conflict, the misery and the confusion one is in. Until one really understands the nature and the structure of this complexity, how one is caught in this trap, there is no freedom—neither the freedom to enquire nor the freedom that comes with great joy in which there is total self-abandonment. Such freedom is not possible if fear exists in any form, either superficially or in the deep recesses of one's mind. We pointed out the relationship between fear, pleasure and desire. To understand fear one must also understand the nature of pleasure.

This morning we shall talk about the centre from which our life and our activities arise and whether it is at all possible to change that centre. Because change, a transformation, an inward revolution, is obviously necessary. To realise that transformation, one must examine very closely what our life is, not escape from it, not indulge in theoretical beliefs and assertions, but observe very closely what our life actually is, and see whether it is possible to transform it completely. In the transformation of it you may affect the nature and the culture of society. There must be change in society, because there are so many evils and social injustices, there is an appalling travesty of worship and so on. But the change in society is of secondary importance; that will come about

naturally, inevitably, when you as a human being in relationship with another, bring about this change in yourself.

This morning we are going to consider three essential
things : what is living?—the life that we lead every day;
what is compassion, love? and the third, what is death?
They are closely related—in understanding the one, we will
understand the other two. As we have seen, you cannot take
fragments of life, choose a part of life you think worthwhile
or which appeals to you, or that your tendency demands.
Either you take the whole of life—in which is involved death,
love and living—or you merely take a fragment of it which
might seem satisfactory, but which will inevitably bring
about greater confusion. So we must take the whole of it and
in considering what living is we must bear in mind that we
are discussing a whole, sane and holy affair.

One observes in the daily life of relationships that there is
conflict, pain and suffering; there is constant dependence on
another, in which there is self-pity and comparison; this is
what we call living. Please let me again repeat : we are not
concerned with theories, we are not propagating any ideology
—for ideologies obviously have no value whatsoever; on the
contrary, they bring about greater confusion, greater conflict.
We are not indulging in opinion, in evaluation, nor in condemnation. We are solely concerned with the observation of
what actually takes place to see if that can be transformed.

One can see very clearly in one's daily life how contradictory, how confused it is; one's life as it is lived now, is
absolutely meaningless. One may invent a meaning; the
intellectuals do invent a meaning and people follow that
meaning—which may be a very clever philosophy, but is
produced out of nothing. Whereas if one is only concerned
with 'what is', without inventing some significance, or escape,
or indulging in theories or ideologies, if one is tremendously
aware, then one's mind is capable of facing 'what is'. Theories
and beliefs do not change one's life—man has had them for
thousands of years and he has not changed; they have, per-

haps, given him a superficial polish; he is, perhaps, less savage, but he is still brutal, violent, capricious, incapable of sustaining seriousness. We live a life of great sorrow from the moment we are born till we die. That is a fact. No amount of speculative theories about that fact will affect it. What does affect 'what is' is the capacity, the energy, the intensity, the passion with which one looks at that fact. And one cannot have passion and intensity, if one's mind is running after some delusion, some speculative ideology.

We are going into something rather complex for which you need all your energy, all your attention—not only while you are here in this hall, but also throughout life, if you are at all serious. What we are concerned with is the changing of 'what is', the sorrow, the conflict, the violence, the dependence on another—not the dependence on the grocer, the doctor, or the postman, but the dependence in our relationship with another, both psychologically and psychosomatically. This dependence on another invariably breeds fear : as long as I depend on you to sustain me, emotionally, psychologically or spiritually, I am your slave and therefore there is fear. This is a fact. Most human beings depend on another and in this dependence there is the self-pity which comes about through comparison. So, where there is psychological dependence on another—on your wife, or on your husband—there must not only be fear and pleasure, but also the pain of it. I hope you are observing this in yourself, and are not merely listening to the speaker.

You know, there are two ways of listening : to listen casually, to hear a series of ideas, agreeing or disagreeing with them; or there is another way of listening, which is not only to listen to the words and the meaning of those words, but also to listen to what is actually taking place in yourself. If you listen in this way, then what the speaker says is related to what you are listening to in yourself; then you are not merely listening to the speaker—which is irrelevant—but to the whole content of your being. And if you are listening in

37

that way with intensity, at the same time and at the same level, then we are both of us partaking, sharing together, in what is actually taking place. Then you have the passion which is going to transform that which is. But if you do not listen that way, with all your mind, with all your heart, then a meeting of this kind becomes utterly meaningless.

In understanding 'what is', the actual, terrible life one leads, one sees that one is leading an isolated life—though one may have a wife and children, yet in oneself there is a self-isolating process going on. The wife, the girl-friend or the boy-friend, each is actually living in isolation; though living together in the same house, each one is isolated, with his own ambitions, with his own fears, with his own sorrow. Living like this is called relationship. Again, this is a fact: you have your image about her and she has her image about you and you have your own image about yourself. The relationship is between these images and is not an actual relationship. So first one must find out how these images are constructed, how they come into being, why they should exist, and what it means to live without such images. I do not know if you have ever considered whether a life in which there is no image, no formula, is possible and what a life without images would mean. We are going to find out.

We have many experiences all the time. We are either conscious or unaware of them. Each experience leaves a mark; these marks build up day after day and they become the image. Someone insults you and at that moment you have already formed the image about the other. Or someone flatters you and again an image is formed. So inevitably each reaction builds an image. And having created it, is it possible to end it?

To end an image we must first find out how it comes into being; and we see that if we do not respond adequately to any challenge it must leave an image. If you call me a fool, immediately you become my enemy, or I do not like you. When you call me a fool I have to be intensely aware at that moment, without any choice, without any condemnation, just listening to what you are saying. If there is no emotional response to your statement, then you will see that no image is being formed.

So one has to be aware of the reaction and not give it time to take root; because the moment that reaction takes root it has formed an image. Now, can you do it? To do it you need attention—not just dreamily wandering through life—attention at the moment of a challenge, with all your being, listening with your heart and with your mind, so that you see clearly what is being said—be it insult or flattery or an opinion about you. Then you will see there is no image at all. The image is always of what has happened in the past. If it is a pleasurable image, we hold on to it. If it is painful, we want to get rid of it. So desire comes into being; one thing we want to hold, the other we want to reject; and desire brings conflict. If you are aware of all this, giving attention to it without any choice, merely observing, then you can find out for yourself, then you are not living according to some psychologist or some priest or some doctor. To find out truth you have to be completely free of all that, to stand alone. And standing alone is to turn your back on society.

If you have observed yourself carefully, you will see that a part of your brain, which has evolved for many thousands of years, is the past—the past being experience, the memory. In that past there is safety. I hope you are watching all this in yourself. The past always responds immediately; and to delay the response of the past when you meet a challenge, so that there is an interval between the challenge and the response, is to end the image. If this does not take place, we will always be living in the past. We *are* the past and there is no freedom in the past. So, that is our life, a constant battle, the past, modified by the present moving into the future—which is still the movement of the past, though modified. As long as this movement exists, man can never be free, he must always be in conflict, in sorrow, in confusion, in misery. Can the response of the past be delayed, so that there is not the immediate formation of an image?

We have to look at life as it is, at the endless confusion and misery and the escape from that into some religious superstition or into the worship of the State, or into various forms of amusement. We have to look at how one escapes into neuroses—because a neurosis offers an extraordinary sense of security. The man who 'believes' is neurotic; the man who worships an image is neurotic. These are neuroses in which there is great safety. And that does not bring about a radical revolution in oneself. To do that you have to observe choicelessly, without any distortion of desire or of pleasure or of fear—just observe actually what you are without escape. And do not name what you see, merely observe. Then you will have the passion, the energy, to observe, and in that observation there comes a tremendous change.

What is love? We talk a great deal about it—love of God, love of humanity, love of country, love of the family—yet strangely, with that love goes hatred. You love your God and hate another's God, you love your nation, your family, but you are against another family, against another nation. And more and more, throughout the world, love is associated with sex. We are not condemning, we are not judging, we are not evaluating; we are merely observing what is actually taking place; and if you know how to observe that gives you tremendous energy.

What is love and what is compassion? The word 'compassion' means passion for everybody, care for everything —including the animals you kill to eat. First let us look at what actually is—not what should be—seeing what actually is, in daily life. Do we know what it means to love, or do we only know pleasure and desire, which we call love?—of course with the pleasure, with the desire, goes tenderness, care, affection and so on. So is love pleasure, desire? Apparently for most of us it is. One depends on one's wife, one loves one's wife, yet if she looks at somebody else, one is angry, frustrated, miserable—and ultimately there is the divorce court. That is what you call love!—and if your wife dies you take another, so great is dependency. One never asks why one depends on another (I am talking about psychological dependency). If you look into it, you will see how lonely you are, deep down, how frustrated and unhappy. You do not know what to do with this loneliness, this isolation, which is a form of suicide. And so, not knowing what to do, you depend. That dependence gives you great comfort and companionship but when that companionship is slightly altered you get jealous, furious.

Would you send your children to war if you loved them? Would you give them the kind of education they have now, only educating them technologically, to help them to get a job, to pass some examinations, and neglect the rest of the whole of this marvellous life? You look after them till they are five so carefully and after that you throw them to the wolves. That is what you call love. Is there love, when there is violence, hatred, antagonism?

So what will you do? Within this violence and hatred is your virtue and your morality; when you deny that, then you are virtuous. That means seeing all the implications of what love is; then you stand alone and you are capable of loving. You listen to this because it is the truth. If you do not live it, truth becomes a poison; if you hear something true and neglect it, that brings about another contradiction in life and therefore more misery. So either listen with your heart and with your complete mind or do not listen at all. But since you are here, you are listening, I hope!

Love is not the opposite of anything. It is not the opposite of hate or of violence. Even if you do not depend on anybody and live a most virtuous life—do social work, demonstrate up and down the street—if you have no love it has no value at all. If you love, then you can do what you will. For the man who loves there is no error—or if there is an error, he corrects it immediately. A man who loves has no jealousy, no remorse; for him there is no forgiveness, because there is not a moment in which a thing that has to be forgiven arises. All this demands deep investigation, great care and attention. But you are caught in the trap of modern society; you have created that trap yourself and if anybody points it out to you, you disregard it. And so wars and hatred go on.

I wonder how you consider death; not theoretically, but actually what it means to you—not as something that is going to come inevitably either through accident, from a disease or from old age. That happens to everybody : old age and the pretensions that go with old age, of trying to be young. All theories, all hope, mean you are in despair; being in despair you look to something to give you hope. Have you ever looked at your despair to see why it exists? It exists because you are comparing yourself with somebody, because you want to fulfil, become, be, achieve.

One of the strange things in life is that we are conditioned by the verb 'to be'. For in that there is the past, the present and the future. All religious conditioning is based on that verb 'to be'; on it are based all heaven and hell, all the beliefs, all the saviours, all the excesses. Can a human being live without that verb—which means to live and to have no past, no future? It does not mean 'living in the present'— you do not know what it means to live in the present. To live completely in the present you must know what the nature and the structure of the past is—which is yourself. You must know yourself so completely, that there is no hidden corner; 'yourself' is the past, and that self thrives on that verb 'to be', to become, to achieve, to remember. Find out what it means to live without that verb psychologically, inwardly.

What does death mean? Why are we all so dreadfully frightened of it? Throughout Asia people believe in re-incarnation; in that there is great hope—I don't know why— and people go on talking and writing about it. When you look at the thing that is going to incarnate, what is it?—all the past, all your misery, all your confusion, all that you are now? And you think the 'you' (here you use the word 'soul') is something permanent. Is there anything in life that is permanent? You would like to have something permanent and so put death into the distance far away from you, never look at it, because you are scared. Then you have 'time'— time between what is and what will inevitably take place.

Either you project your life into tomorrow and continue as you are now, hoping that there will be some kind of resurrection, incarnation, or you die each day; die each day to yourself, to your misery, to your sorrow; you put aside that burden each day so that your mind is fresh, young and innocent. The word 'innocence' means 'incapable of being hurt'. To have a mind that is not capable of being hurt, does not mean that it has built up a lot of resistance—on the contrary, such a mind is dying to everything that it has known in which there has been conflict, pleasure and pain. Only then is the mind innocent; that means it can love. You cannot love with memory, love is not a matter of remembrance, of time.

So love, death and living, are not separate but a total whole, and there is sanity. Sanity is not possible when there is hate, anger, jealousy, when there is dependency which breeds fear. Where there is sanity, life becomes holy; there is great joy and you can do what you will; what you do then is virtuous, is true.

We do not know all this—we only know our misery—and not knowing, we try to escape. If only we did not escape, but could actually observe, never moving away even a fraction from 'what is' by naming it, by condemning or judging it— but could just watch it. To watch something you need care —care means compassion. A life that is lived so splendidly and completely can then go into something we shall talk about tomorrow, which is meditation. Without laying such a foundation, meditation is self-hypnosis. Laying this foundation means that you have understood this extraordinary life, so you have a mind that is without conflict and you lead a life that has compassion, beauty and therefore order. Not the order of a blueprint, but the order which comes when you understand what disorder is—which is your life. Your life *is* in disorder. Disorder is contradiction, the conflict between opposites. When you understand that disorder which is in yourself, then out of that comes order—the order which is precise, mathematical, in which there is no distortion. All this demands a meditative mind, a mind that is capable of looking silently.

Questioner: In one of your books you say that miracles are one of the easiest things to do. Will you please explain about the miracles you mentioned.

KRISHNAMURTI : I wish you would not quote from a book—including the speaker's. (*Laughter.*) I really mean it, seriously. Do not quote anybody. Living on other people's ideas is one of the most terrible things to do. And ideas are not truth. 'In one of the books it is said that miracles are the easiest things in the world'—are they not? Is it not a miracle that you are sitting there and I here and we are talking to each other? Because if you listen without effort you will know what it means to live completely, wholly; if you live that way, there is a miracle, the greatest miracle of all.

Questioner: I have been away for twenty-seven years and have come back about three months ago. I find tremendous fears developing here. From my own observation and from the observation of my friends I believe there is the take-over of the Mafia and the development of a complete police state. Can you help us as individuals, give us the key to fight against such conditions? I realise that to fight will be difficult, I also realise that if we fight we could go to jail. What can each individual do for himself to combat these awful forces?

KRISHNAMURTI : Sir, this is not an avoidance of the question, but : can you as an individual be peaceful? Are you an individual at all? You may have your bank account, you may have a separate house, a separate family and so on, but are you an individual? Individual means indivisible in himself, not fragmented. But we are fragmented, broken up, so we are not individuals. What society is, we are. We have made this society. So how can a broken-up human being do anything but come to that state in which he is completely whole? Then a totally different kind of action will take place. But as long as we are acting in fragments, we are bound to create more chaos in the world. I am sure this answer satisfies nobody; you want the key and the key is in yourself. You have to forge that key.

Questioner: But time is short and I do not seem to be able to find out how exactly to go about this.

KRISHNAMURTI : 'Time is short'—can you change immediately? Not change gradually or tomorrow. Can you have this perception of a 'whole' life in which there is love—all that we have talked about this morning—immediately? The speaker says that is the only thing to do—to change completely, radically, immediately. To do that, you have to observe with all your heart and mind; not escaping into anything, nationalism or your beliefs; put all these aside with one breath and become completely aware. Then there is a radical change, immediately, and from that immediate transformation you will act completely differently.

Questioner: Does love have an object? Can one love only one person in one's life?

KRISHNAMURTI : Have you heard the question? Can you love one at the same time as the many? What a strange question to ask. If you love, you love the one and the many. But we do not love. Sir, many can smell a flower that has perfume —or only one can smell it—but the flower does not care, it is there. And that is the beauty of love : it can give to one or to many. That is only possible when there is compassion, when there is no jealousy, no ambition, no success; and that is the denial of all that man has built in himself or around himself. Through negation the positive comes into being.

Santa Monica, California. 7 March 1970.

4

RELIGION

'Religion, then, is something that cannot possibly be put into words; it cannot be measured by thought . . .'

W E   S A I D   W E would talk about religion and meditation this evening. They form a really quite complex subject, needing a great deal of patience and hesitant enquiry, never assuming anything, never accepting or believing anything. Man has always sought something more than the daily living, with its pain, pleasure and sorrow; he has always wanted to find something more permanent. And in his search for this unnameable thing, he has built temples, churches, mosques. Extraordinary things have been done in the name of religion. There have been wars for which religions are responsible; people have been tortured, burned, destroyed; for belief was more important than truth, dogma more vital than the direct perception. When belief becomes all-important, then you are willing to sacrifice everything for that; whether that belief is real or has no vailidity does not matter as long as it gives comfort, security, a sense of permanency.

It is very easy, if you seek something, to find it; but that means that before one begins to search one must have a basis, an idea of what is sought. In seeking, there are several processes involved; there is not only the desire and the hope that what you recognise will be the truth, but there is also the motive behind that search. If there is a motive of escape from fear, a longing for comfort and security, then you will inevitably find something that will gratify you; it may be the most absurd belief, but as long as it is satisfactory and completely comforting, however ridiculous the illusion be, you cling to it. So there is great danger for those who are seeking to find.

If there is fear of any kind, hidden or open, searching becomes an evasion, a flight from the actual. And if in your search you discover something, that discovery is based on recognition—you must recognise it, otherwise it has no value. But recognition, if you observe, is of past memory, of something you have already known, otherwise you cannot possibly recognise it. All this is involved in this everlasting search for what one considers to be the truth; but some thing that is beyond the measure of the mind, is not based on recognition.

Religion, in the accepted sense of that word, has now become a matter of propaganda, of vested interest, with much property, with a great hierarchical, bureaucratic system of 'spirituality'. Religion has become a matter of dogma, belief and ritual—something which is totally divorced from daily living. You may, or you may not, believe in God, but that belief has very little meaning in daily life, where you cheat, where you destroy, are ambitious, greedy, jealous, violent. You believe in God or in a saviour, or in some guru, yet keep that far away so that it does not actually touch your daily life.

Religion, as it is now, has become an extraordinary phenomenon which has no validity at all. The Christian, for the last two thousand years, has been conditioned to believe. Please observe in yourself, not criticising, not condemning, just observing. One may not like it, but one must face the fact that one is, if one is a Christian, as conditioned as the Communist or the atheist. The believer and the non-believer are both conditioned by the culture of their time, by society, by the extraordinary process of propaganda. It has also been going on in Asia for thousands of years.

All the physical structure, the psychological assertions, the strong beliefs, for which one is willing to destroy and be destroyed, are based on dialectical, assertive opinion, as to how to find out what is true; but 'true opinion', however clever, however argumentative, has no reality whatsoever: it remains merely an opinion. Religions throughout the world now are utterly meaningless. We want to be entertained spiritually and so we go to the church or the temple or the mosque and that has nothing whatsoever to do with our daily sorrow, confusion and hatred. A man who is really serious, who really wants to find out if there is something more than this terrible thing called existence, must obviously be completely free from dogma, from belief, from propaganda, he must be free from the structure in which he has been brought up to be a 'religious man'.

Through the negation of 'what is', in the so-called religions, you come to the positive. We are going to find out, if we can, what the thing is that man has sought—not through any belief, not through any saviour or through a guru, or through the speaker. We are going to find out for ourselves if there is, or if there is not, something that is not the projection of one's own hopes, of one's own fears, something that is not invented by a cunning mind or is bred from our intense loneliness.

To find out, one must be free of belief; for belief is the quality of mind that invests in something that will give it some hope, comfort, security, a sense of permanency. To be free to enquire, one must be free from fear, from anxiety, from the desire to be psychologically secure. These are the obvious requirements for a very earnest and serious person who wants to find out.

The instrument that is capable of enquiry is a mind that is clear, that has no distortions, or prejudice of conclusion, of formula, or belief. See how extraordinarily difficult it is to have a mind that is not in conflict; for it means a mind that has understood conflict and is free from it.

The mind—which means not only the mind but also the heart, the whole psychosomatic nature of man—must be highly sensitive; for sensitivity implies intelligence. We are going to go into that a little, because all this is laying the foundation for meditation. If you do not lay the foundation of order, then meditation—which is one of the most extraordinary things in life—becomes merely an escape leading to self-delusion, self-hypnosis. A shoddy mind can learn the tricks, can practise so-called meditation, but it will still remain a shoddy, stupid mind.

Most of us have very little energy; we spend it in conflict, in struggle, we waste it in various manners—not only sexually, but also a great deal of it is wasted in contradictions and in the fragmentation of ourselves which brings about conflict. Conflict is definitely a great waste of energy—the 'voltage' decreases. Not only is physical energy necessary, but so also is psychological energy, with a mind that is immensely clear, logical, healthy, undistorted, and a heart that has no sentiment whatsoever, no emotion, but the quality of abundance of love, of compassion. All this gives a great intensity, passion. You need that, otherwise you cannot take a journey into this thing called meditation. You may sit cross-legged, breathe, do fantastic things, but you will never come to it.

The body must be extraordinarily sensitive; that is one of the most difficult things, because we have spoiled the intelligence of the body through drink, through smoking, through indulgence, through pleasure; we have made the body coarse. Look at the body which should be extraordinarily alive and sensitive, and you will see what we have reduced it to! The body affects the mind and the mind affects the body, and for this reason, sensitivity of the body, the organism, is essential. This sensitivity is not brought about through fasting, through playing all kinds of tricks on it. The mind has to watch it dispassionately. (I hope you are doing it now, as the speaker is going into the problem—not tomorrow or the next day—because as we said, we are partaking together in the journey, in the exploration).

Observation of 'what is', is the understanding of that event. Understanding is derived from the observation of 'what is'; testing it out in everyday living leads to the understanding of experience. Most of us want great experiences because our own lives are so limited, so unspeakably dull. We want deep, lasting, beautiful experiences. But we have not even understood what that word 'experience' means, and the mind that is seeking an experience is incapable of understanding what truth is. The life that we lead every day has to be transformed; there must be an end to this hatred, this violence in oneself, the anxiety, the guilt, the drive to succeed, to be somebody; and without changing all that radically, to try to seek some 'experience' has no meaning whatsoever.

A mind that hopes to see truth through drugs, to have extraordinary experiences, or to be entertained through drugs, becomes a slave to them and they ultimately make the mind dull and stupid.

We are inquiring together into the question of the religious mind—not what religion is—but what a mind is that is religious, that is capable of finding out truth. The root meaning of the word 'religion' is rather uncertain; we can give any meaning to it we like, and we generally do. But to have no opinion of what religion is, is to be free to enquire into it, into the quality of the mind that is religious. That quality of mind is not separated from the daily living of pain, pleasure, sorrow and confusion.

To enquire into this, there must be freedom from all authority. You are alone to find out, there is no book, nobody to help you. Please see how important this is, because we have given our trust, our faith to others—to the priest, to the saviours, to the teachers and so on—and having given over our faith, we have looked to them to lead us and they have led us nowhere.

In this enquiry there is no question of authority—you are enquiring, like a true scientist, without seeking a result. When there is no authority whatsoever, then there is no system, no practice. A system, a method, implies a routine, a forming of habit. If you practise a certain system daily, your mind invariably becomes dull. This is so simple and obvious. So

51

systems, methods, practices, must completely disappear. See what is happening to a mind that is not afraid, that is not seeking pleasure or pursuing entertainment, a mind that has no dependence on authority, but is really enquiring; to a mind that does not depend on anything there is no fear and therefore it can enquire. Such a mind has already become extraordinarily sharp, alive, intense, earnest. (When we use the word 'mind', we mean the whole of it, including the organism, the heart.) That quality of mind has beauty; using no method, it is clear, enquiring, observing and learning as it is observing. Learning is not different from action. To learn is to act. If you learn about nationality, the dangers of separation, of division of people, if you observe it and understand it, then the very understanding of it puts an end to this division in action. So observation is astonishingly important.

You probably all know about yoga. There are so many books written about it, every Tom, Dick and Harry who has spent some months in India and taken a few lessons, becomes a 'yogi'. That word 'yoga' has many meanings; it implies a way of life, not just the practising of some exercises to keep young. It implies a way of life in which there is no division and therefore no conflict—which is the way the speaker looks at it. Of course regular exercise of the right kind is good, it keeps the body supple. The speaker has done a great deal of it for years, not to achieve some extraordinary state through breathing and all the rest of it, but to keep the body supple. You must have the right kind of exercise, the right food, not stuffing yourself with a lot of meat—with all the brutality and insensitivity that that inevitably brings about. Each one has to find out the right diet for himself, he has to experiment and test it out.

Then there is this trick that has been foisted on you: Mantra Yoga. For five, or thirty dollars, you have been taught some mantra—a repetition of words, especially in Sanskrit. The Catholics have a rosary and repeat Ave Maria—or whatever they repeat. Do you know what happens when you constantly repeat a series of words? You mesmerise yourself into tranquillity. Or you ride on the tone of the word. When you keep on repeating a certain word it produces a sound, inwardly; and that inward sound keeps going—if you listen to it; it becomes extraordinarily alive and you think that is a most marvellous thing. It is nothing of the kind, it is a form of self-hypnosis. That too has to be rejected completely.

Then we come to something quite different, which is: awareness and attention. I do not know if you have gone into this—not by reading books, not by being taught how to be aware in a school in Asia, in some monastery—but if you have, you will see for yourself what it means not to be taught by another. You have to learn for yourself what awareness means; to be aware of the hall in which you are sitting, to be aware of the proportion of the hall and the colours that it contains; not saying it is ugly or beautiful, just observing. As you walk down the street, be aware of the things that are happening around you, observing the clouds, the trees, the light on the water, the bird in flight. Be aware without any interference by thought which says: 'this is right', 'this is wrong', 'this should be', or 'should not be'. Be aware of the things that are happening outside, then also be aware inwardly—watch every movement of thought, watch every feeling, every reaction; that makes the mind extraordinarily alive.

There is a difference between concentration and attention. Concentration is a process of exclusion, a process of resistance and therefore a conflict. Have you ever watched your mind when you are trying to concentrate on something? It wanders off and you try to pull it back and so a battle goes on; you want to focus your attention, to concentrate on something, and thought is interested in looking out of the window, or in thinking about something else. In this conflict there is such a waste of energy and time.

One enquires why the mind chatters, talks endlessly to itself or to somebody else, or wants to be occupied everlastingly, in reading a book, turning on the radio, keeping active. Why? If you have observed, there is a habit of restlessness, your body can never sit still for any prolonged time, it is always doing something or fidgeting. The mind also chatters; otherwise what would happen to it?—it is frightened, so it must be occupied. It must be occupied with social reform, with this or that, with some belief, with some quarrel, with something that has happened in the past—it is thinking constantly.

As we were saying: attention is entirely different from concentration. Awareness and attention go together—but not concentration. A mind that is intensely attentive can observe very clearly, without any distortion, without any resistance, and yet function efficiently, objectively. What is the quality of such a mind? (I hope you are interested in this, because it is part of life. If you reject all this, you reject the whole of life also. If you do not know the meaning and the beauty of meditation you do not know anything of life. You may have the latest car, you may be able to travel all over the world freely, but if you do not know what the real beauty, the freedom and the joy of meditation is, you are missing a great part of life. Which is not to make you say, 'I must learn to meditate'. It is a natural thing that comes about. A mind that is enquiring must inevitably come to this; a mind that is aware, that observes 'what is' in itself, is self-understanding, self-knowing.)

We are asking: what is the quality of a mind that has come so far, naturally, without any effort? If you look at a tree or a cloud, the face of your wife or your husband or your neighbour, it is only out of silence that you can observe very clearly. You can only listen when there is no self-projected noise. When you are chattering to yourself, comparing what is being said with what you already know, then you are not listening. When you are observing with your eyes and all kinds of prejudices and knowledge are interfering, you are not really observing. So when you really observe and listen, you can only do so out of silence.

I do not know if you have ever gone that far. It is not something you cultivate, take years to come upon, because it is not the product of time or of comparison; it is the product of observation in daily life, the observation of your thoughts and the understanding of thought. *When the mind is completely aware it becomes extraordinarily silent, quiet; it is not asleep, but highly awake in that silence.* Only such a mind can see what truth is, can see if there is something beyond or not. Only such a mind is a religious mind, because it has left the past completely—though it can use the memory of the past. Religion then is something that cannot possibly be put into words; it cannot be measured by thought—for thought *is* always measuring; it is, as we said, the response of the past. Thought is never free; it is always functioning within the field of the known.

So a mind that is capable of understanding what truth is, what reality is—if there is such a thing as reality—must be completely free of all the human tricks, deceptions and illusions. And this takes a lot of work. It means an inward discipline; a discipline which is not imitation, conformity or adjustment. Discipline comes in the observaton of 'what is' and learning about it; this learning about itself is its own discipline. Therefore there is order and with it the end of disorder in oneself. All this, from the beginning of these talks till now, is part of meditation.

Only if you know how to look at a cloud or see the beauty of the light on the sea, how to look at your wife—or the boy, or the girl—with a fresh eye, with an innocent mind that has never been harmed, that has never shed a tear, can the mind see what truth is.

Questioner: A while ago I had verified for myself what you say—that the key to inner freedom is to experience that the observer and observed are one. I had very laborious and tedious work to perform, for which I developed a great resistance. I realised that I was this resistance and that only resistance looked at resistance. Then suddenly that resistance was gone—it was like a miracle—and I had even physical strength to finish my work.

KRISHNAMURTI: Are you trying to confirm what I am saying, giving me or the audience encouragement? (*Laughter.*)

Questioner: It needs enormous energy before one comes to the point of seeing that observer and observed are one.

KRISHNAMURTI: The gentleman says that the observer is the observed; that is: when there is fear, the observer is part of that fear. He is not identifying himself with fear; the observer is part of that very fear itself. To realise that is fairly simple. Either you realise it verbally, theoretically— understanding the meaning of the words—or you actually see that the observer and the observed are one. If you see that actually, it does make a drastic difference in your life; it ends conflict. When there is a division between the observer and the observed, a gap, there is a time-interval, and therefore there is conflict. When you actually see and test by observing that the observer and the observed are actually one, then you end all conflict in life, in all relationships.

Questioner: When we realise that the past, as the memory, is interposed between something deeper and the outside, what can we do? We cannot stop it—it keeps going on.

KRISHNAMURTI: The memory interposes itself between the outer and the inner. There is the inner, and the outer, and the mind as memory as something separate, as the past. So there are three things now, the inner, the outer, and the mind as the past. Please, sir, do not laugh—this is our life, this is what we are doing; though you may put the question differently, this is actually what is going on in our daily life. You want to do something; the mind says, 'Do not do it, or, do it some other way', so there is a battle going on. The mind is interfering; the mind as the thought, thought being the past. Thought comes in between the actual, the inner and the outer; so what is one to do? The function of thought is to divide; it has divided life as the past, the present, and the future. Thought has also divided the inner from the outer. Thought says: 'How can I bridge the two and act as a whole'. Can thought do this?—being itself the factor of division?

Questioner: Where there is a will there is a way.

KRISHNAMURTI: No, sir: you have your way in the world; you have your will to destroy people and you have succeeded, you have found the way. We are not concerned with will; will is the most destructive thing, for will is based on pleasure, on desire, and not on free joy.

You are asking how thought can be kept quiet. How can thought be silent? Is that the right question?—because if you put the wrong question you invariably get the wrong answer. (*Laughter.*) No, sir, this is not a laughing matter. You must put the right question. Is it the right question to ask: 'How can thought end'? Or must one find out what the function of thought is? If you put an end to thought—if that is at all possible—then how will you operate when you have to go to the office? Thought, apparently, is necessary.

We are saying thought is dangerous in a certain direction, because it divides; and yet thought must function logically, sanely, objectively, healthily, in another direction. How is this possible? How can thought not interfere? You see the problem? It is not 'how to end thought'. When you have put the question very clearly, you will see it for yourself. Thought, which is the response of the past, interferes, divides as the outer and the inner and destroys unity. So we say, 'Let us destroy thought, let us kill the mind.' This is a totally wrong question. But if you enquired into the whole structure of thought, saw what its place is, where it is not necessary, then you would find out that mind will operate intelligently when thought does not function as also when thought must function.

Questioner: Why is it that you have a greater awareness of 'what is' than I have? What is your secret?

KRISHNAMURTI: I have really never thought about it. Just look: is humility something to be cultivated? If you cultivate humility, it is still vanity. If you cultivate awareness of 'what is', you are not being aware. But if you are aware when you sit in a bus, or drive a car, when you look, talk, or are enjoying yourself, then out of that, naturally, easily, comes the awareness of 'what is'. *But if you try to cultivate paying a great deal of attention to 'what is', thought is operating, not awareness.*

Questioner: Did you say: to be free we should have no teachers? Did I understand it rightly!

KRISHNAMURTI: What is the function of a teacher? If he knows a subject like medicine, science, how to run a computer and so on, his function is to instruct another about the knowledge and the information he has. That is fairly simple. But if we are talking about the teacher who says he knows, and wants to instruct the disciple, then be suspicious, for the man who says he knows, does not know. Because truth, the beauty of enlightenment, whatever you call it, cannot ever be described—it is. It is a living thing, a moving thing, it is active, it is weightless. Only about a dead thing can you say what it is; and the teacher who teaches you about dead things is not a teacher.

Questioner: How can we put concentration, discipline and attention together?

KRISHNAMURTI : The word 'discipline' means to learn from another. The disciple is one who learns from the teacher. Have you ever considered or gone into the question of what learning is? The active present of the verb 'to learn'—what does it mean? Either you are learning in order to add to what you already know, which becomes knowledge—like science—or there is learning which is not an accumulation of knowledge but a movement. Do you see the difference between the two? I either learn in order to acquire knowledge, to be efficient, technologically and so on, or I am learning all the time something which is always new and therefore action is always new. Please listen to this : I want to know, I want to learn about myself. I am a very complex entity, there is both the hidden and the obvious. I want to know about the whole totality of myself. So I watch myself and I see I am afraid; I see the cause of that fear; in watching I have learnt and that has become my knowledge. But if the next time fear arises, I look at it with the previous knowledge, then I have stopped learning. I am only looking at it with the past and am not learning about what is actually going on. To learn about myself, there must be freedom, so that there is constant observation without the past interfering—without thought interfering.

So 'learning' has two meanings : learning to acquire knowledge with which I can operate most efficiently in certain fields, or learning about oneself, so that the past—which is thought—does not interfere all the time; in that way I can observe, and the mind is always sensitive.

Questioner: I would like to ask you if you eat meat or fish?

KRISHNAMURTI : Does it really interest you? All my life I have never touched meat or fish—I have never tasted it, have never smoked or drunk; it does not appeal, there is no meaning to it. Will that make you also a vegetarian? (*Laughter.*) It won't! You know, heroes, examples, are the worst things you can have. Find out why you eat meat, why you indulge in smoking and drinking, why you cannot lead a simple life—which does not mean one suit of clothes, or one meal a day, but a quality of mind that is simple, without all the distortions of pleasures and desires, ambitions and motives —so that you can look directly and perceive the beauty of the world.

Questioner: I just wanted to ask what humour is.

KRISHNAMURTI : I suppose it means really, to laugh at oneself. We have so many tears in our hearts, so much misery— just to look at ourselves with laughter, to observe with clarity, with seriousness and yet with laughter, if one can.

Santa Monica, California. 8 March 1970.

PART II

5

FEAR

'Can you observe without the centre, not naming the thing called fear as it arises? It requires tremendous discipline.'

O N E H A S T O be serious, for only those who are vitally serious can live a life that is complete and whole. And that seriousness does not exclude joy, enjoyment; yet as long as there is fear one cannot possibly know what it means to have great joy. Fear seems to be one of the most common things in life; strangely we have accepted it as a way of life—just as we have accepted violence in all its various forms as a way of life—and we have become used to being psychologically afraid.

We should, I feel, go into the question of fear completely, understand it fully, so that when we leave this place we shall be rid of it. It can be done; it is not just a theory, or a hope. If one gives complete attention to this question of fear, to how one approaches it, looks at it, then one will find that the mind —the mind that has suffered so much, that has endured so much pain, that has lived with great sorrow and fear—will be completely free of it. To go into this it is absolutely essential that one has no prejudice which will prevent one from understanding the truth of 'what is'. To take this journey together implies neither acceptance nor denial; neither saying to oneself that it is absolutely impossible to be rid of fear, nor that it is possible. One needs a free mind to enquire into this question; a mind that, having reached no conclusion, is free to observe, to enquire.

There are so many forms of psychological and psychosomatic fear. To go into each one of these various forms of fear, into every aspect, would take an enormous amount of time. But one can observe the general quality of fear; one can observe the general nature and structure of fear without getting lost in the detail of a particular form of one's fears. When one understands the nature and structure of fear as such, then one can approach, with that understanding, the particular fear.

One may be afraid of the dark; one may be afraid of one's wife or husband, or of what the public says or thinks or does; one may be afraid of the sense of loneliness, or of the emptiness of life, the boredom of the meaningless existence that one leads. One may be afraid of the future, of the uncertainty and insecurity of tomorrow—or of the bomb. One may be afraid of death, the ending of one's life. There are so many forms of fear, the neurotic as well as the sane rational fears— if fear can ever be rational or sane. Most of us are neurotically afraid of the past, of today and of tomorrow; so that time is involved in fear.

There are not only the conscious fears of which one is aware, but also those that are deep down, undiscovered in the deep recesses of one's mind. How is one to deal with conscious fears as well as those that are hidden? Surely fear is in the movement away from 'what is'; it is the flight, the escape, the avoidance of actually 'what is'; it is this flight away that brings about fear. Also, when there is comparison, of any kind, there is the breeding of fear—the comparison of what you are with what you think you should be. So fear is in the movement away from what is actual, not in the object from which you move away.

None of these problems of fear can be resolved through will—saying to oneself, 'I will not be afraid.' Such acts of will have no meaning.

We are considering a very serious problem to which one has to give one's complete attention. One cannot give attention if one is interpreting or translating or comparing what is being said with what one already knows. One has to listen—an art one has to learn, for normally one is always comparing, evaluating, judging, agreeing, denying, and one does not listen at all; actually one prevents oneself from listening. To listen so completely implies that one gives one's whole attention—it does not mean one agrees or disagrees. There is no agreement or disagreement when we are exploring together; but the 'microscope' through which one looks may not be clear. If one looks through a precision instrument then what one sees is what another will also see; therefore there is no question of agreement or disagreement. In trying to examine this whole question of fear one has to give one's whole attention; and yet, until fear is resolved it deadens the mind, makes it insensitive, dull.

How does it happen that the hidden fears are exposed? One can know the conscious fears—how to deal with them will come presently—but there are hidden fears which are perhaps much more important. So how will one deal with them, how will one expose them? Can they be exposed through analysis, seeking their cause? Will analysis free the mind from fear, not a particular neurotic fear, but the whole structure of fear? In analysis is implied, not only time but the analyser—taking many, many days, years, even the whole of one's life, at the end of which perhaps you have understood a little, but you are ready for the grave. Who is the analyser? If he is the professional, the expert who has a degree, he will also take time; he also is the result of many forms of conditioning. If one analyses oneself there is implied the analyser, who is the censor, and he is going to analyse the fear which he himself has created. In any event analysis takes time; in the interval between that which you are analysing and its ending many other factors will arise which give it a different direction. You have to see the truth that analysis is not the way, because the analyser is a fragment among the many other fragments which go to make up the 'me', the I, the ego—he is the result of time, he is conditioned. To see that analysis implies time and does not bring the ending of fear means that you have completely put aside the whole idea of progressive change; you have seen that the very factor of change is one of the major causes of fear.

(To me, to the speaker, this is a very important thing, therefore he feels very strongly, he speaks intensely; but he is not doing propaganda—there is nothing for you to join, nothing for you to believe; but observe and learn and be free of this fear.)

So analysis is not the way. When you see the truth of that, it means you are no longer thinking in terms of the analyser who is going to analyse, going to judge and evaluate, and your mind is free of that particular burden called analysis; therefore it is capable of looking directly.

How are you to look at this fear; how are you to bring out all its structure, all its hidden parts?—through dreams? Dreams are the continuation of the activity of waking hours during sleep—are they not? You observe in dreams that there is always action, something or other is happening in dreams as in the waking hours, a continuation which is still part of one whole movement. So dreams have no value. You see what is happening : we are eliminating the things to which you are accustomed, analysis, dreams, will, time; when you eliminate all those, the mind becomes extraordinarily sensitive—not only sensitive but intelligent. Now with that sensitivity and intelligence we are going to look at fear. (If you really go into this, you turn your back on the whole of the social structure in which time, analysis and will is in operation.) What is fear?—how does it come? Fear is always in relation to something; it does not exist by itself. There is fear of what happened yesterday in relation to the possibility of its repetition tomorrow; there is always a fixed point from which relationship takes place. How does fear come into this? I had pain yesterday; there is the memory of it and I do not want it again tomorrow. *Thinking* about the pain of yesterday, thinking which involves the memory of yesterday's pain, projects the fear of having pain again tomorrow. So it is thought that brings about fear. Thought breeds fear; thought also cultivates pleasure. To understand fear you must also understand pleasure—they are interrelated; without understanding one you cannot understand the other; this means that one cannot say 'I must have only pleasure and no fear'; fear is the other side of the coin which is called pleasure.

Thinking with the images of yesterday's pleasure, thought imagines that you may not have that pleasure tomorrow—so thought engenders fear. Thought tries to sustain pleasure and thereby nourishes fear.

Thought has separated itself as the analyser and the thing to be analysed—they are both parts of thought playing tricks upon itself. In doing all this it is refusing to examine the unconscious fears; it brings in time as a means of escaping fear and yet at the same time sustains fear.

Thought nourishes pleasure—which has nothing whatever to do with joy; joy is not the product of thought, it is not pleasure. You can cultivate pleasure, you can think about it endlessly; you cannot do that with joy. The moment you think about joy it has gone, it has become something from which you derive pleasure and therefore something which you are afraid to lose.

Thought engenders loneliness but condemns it and so invents ways of escaping from it, through various forms of religious or cultural entertainment, through the everlasting search for deeper and wider dependencies.

Thought is responsible for all these daily observable facts; they are not the speaker's invention, or his peculiar philosophy or theory. What is one to do? You cannot kill thought, you cannot destroy it, you cannot say, 'I'll forget it', you cannot resist it; if you do, it is again the action of another form of thought.

Thought is the response of memory: that memory is needed to function in daily life, to go to your office, your home, to be able to talk; memory is the storehouse of technological knowledge. So you need memory and yet you see how memory through thought sustains fear. Memory is needed in all purity and clarity of thought in one direction—technologically, to function daily, to earn a livelihood and so on—and yet you see the fact that it also breeds fear. So what is the mind to do? How will you answer this question, after having gone through the various facts of analysis, of time, of escape, of dependency, having seen how the movement away from 'what is' is fear; the movement itself is fear? After observing all that, seeing the truth of all that—not as opinion, not as your casual judgment—what is your answer to this question? How can thought function efficiently, sanely and yet that very thought not become a danger, because it breeds fear?

What is that state of the mind that has gone through all this? What state of understanding has the mind, that has examined all these various factors which we have exposed, which have been explained or observed?—what is the quality of your mind now?—because on that quality depends your answer. If you have actually taken the journey, step by step, and gone into everything that we have discussed, then your mind, you will see, has become extraordinarily intelligent, live and sensitive, because it has thrown off all the burden that it had accumulated. How do you now observe the whole process of thinking? Is there a centre from which you think? —the centre being the censor, the one who judges, evaluates, condemns, justifies. Do you still think from that centre?—or is there no centre from which to think at all, yet there is thought? Do you see the difference?

Thought has created a centre as the 'me'—'me', my opinion, my country, my God, my experience, my house, my furniture, my wife, my children, you know, 'me', 'me', 'me'. That is the centre from which you act. That centre divides. That centre and that division are the cause of conflict, obviously—when it is your opinion against somebody else's opinion, my country, your country, that is all division created by thought. You observe from that centre and you are still caught in fear, because that centre has separated itself from the thing it has called fear; it says, 'I must get rid of it,' 'I must analyse it', 'I must overcome it', 'resist it' and so on; thereby you are strengthening fear.

Can the mind look at fear without the centre?—can you look at that fear without naming it?—the moment you name it 'fear', it is already in the past. The moment you name something, you divide it off. So, can you observe without that centre, not naming the thing called fear, as it arises? It requires tremendous discipline. Then the mind is looking without the centre to which it has been accustomed and there is the ending of fear, both the hidden and the open.

If you have not seen the truth of it this evening, do not take it home as a problem to think about. Truth is something which you must see immediately—and to see something clearly you must give your heart and your mind and your whole being to it immediately.

Questioner: Are you saying that, rather than trying to escape from fear—what is in essence fearing fear—we should accept fear?

KRISHNAMURTI: No, sir. Do not accept anything. Do not accept fear but look at it. You have never looked at fear, have you? You have never said, 'Well, I am afraid, let me look.' Rather you have said, 'I am afraid, let me turn on the radio'—or go to Church or pick up a book, or resort to a belief—any movement away. Having never looked at fear you have never come directly into communication with it; you have never looked at fear without naming it, without running away, without trying to overcome it. Just be with it, without any movement away from it and if you do this, you will see a very strange thing happen.

Questioner: After you meet fear, can you become it?

KRISHNAMURTI : You are fear; how can you become it? You are fear, only thought has separated itself from the fear, not knowing what to do with it, resisting it; dividing itself from fear it becomes the 'observer' of that fear which resists or escapes from it. But the 'observer', that which resists, is also fear.

Questioner: Sir, a great deal of frustration exists because people are not permitted to tape-record lectures, privately. Could you tell us why, please?

KRISHNAMURTI : I will tell you—it is very simple. First of all : if you are taking a recording of this talk, it is very disturbing to your neighbour—you are fiddling with the instrument, all the rest of it. Secondly, what is more important : to listen, directly, now, to what is being said, or to take home a recording and listen to it at leisure? When the speaker is saying, 'Do not allow time to interfere', you say, on the contrary, 'Well, I'll record what you are saying and take it home.' Surely fear is now; you have it in your heart, in your mind, now.

Questioner: If that is true then why does the Foundation sell tapes?

KRISHNAMURTI : Is that not the most important thing : to listen directly to what is being said now, while you are here? You have taken all the trouble to come here and the speaker has taken all the trouble to come here also. We are trying to communicate together, trying to understand something now, not tomorrow. And the understanding 'now' is of the highest importance, therefore you must give all your attention to it.

You cannot give all your attention if you are taking notes, if you are giving half your attention to a tape recorder. You may not understand all this immediately, so you may want to listen to it again. Then buy a tape, or do not buy a tape, a book or not a book—that is all. If you can take in all that has been said this evening during an hour and ten minutes, completely, so that you absorb it wholly, with your heart and mind, it is finished. You have not done it, unfortunately; you have not given your mind to all this before; you have accepted fear, you have lived with fear and your fear has become your habit. What the speaker is saying is to shatter all that. And the speaker says, 'Do it now, not tomorrow'. Our minds are not used to seeing the total nature of fear and what is implied in it. But if you could see it immediately, you would leave this hall with ecstatic mind. But most of us are not capable of it, and therefore the tapes.

Questioner: You observe fear and find yourself moving away from it. What are you to do?

KRISHNAMURTI: First of all, do not resist moving away. To observe fear you must give attention, and in attention you are not condemning, not judging, not evaluating, but just observing. When you move away, it is because your attention has wandered, you are not attending—there is inattention. Be inattentive, but be aware that you are inattentive—that very awareness of your inattention is attention. If you are aware of your inattention, be aware of it, do not do anything about it, except be aware that you are inattentive; then that very awareness is attention. It is so simple. Once you see this you will eliminate conflict altogether; you are aware without choice. When you say, 'I have been attentive, but now I am not attentive and I must become attentive', there is choice. To be aware means to be aware without choice.

Questioner: If, as you say, fear and pleasure are related, can one remove fear and so enjoy pleasure completely?

KRISHNAMURTI : Lovely, wouldn't it be? Take away all my fears so that I can enjoy myself in my pleasures. Everybody right through the world wants the same thing, some very crudely, some very subtly—to escape fear and hold on to pleasure. Pleasure—you smoke, it is a pleasure, yet there is pain within it because you may get a disease. You have had pleasure, whether as man or woman, sexually or otherwise, comfort and so on : when the other looks away you are jealous, angry, frustrated, mutilated.

Pleasure inevitably brings pain (we are not saying we cannot have pleasure); but see the whole structure and you will know then that joy, real enjoyment, the beauty of enjoyment, the freedom of it, has nothing whatsoever to do with pleasure or therefore with pain or fear. If you see that, the truth of it, then you will understand pleasure and give it its proper place.

San Diego State College. 6 April 1970.

72

6

VIOLENCE

'As long as the "me" survives in any form, very subtly
or grossly, there must be violence.'

W HAT SHALL WE discuss this morning? The word 'dis-
cussion' is not right, it is more a dialogue. Opinions will lead
us nowhere and indulging in mere intellectual cleverness will
have very little meaning, because truth is not to be found
through the exchange of opinions or of ideas. So if we are to
talk over together any problem it must be on the level which
is not intellectual, emotional or sentimental.

Questioner: I think the war against Communism is in a cer-
tain sense justified. I would like to find out with you if I am
right or wrong. You must understand, I lived ten years under
Communism, I was in a Russian concentration camp, I was
also in a Communist prison. They understand only one langu-
age which is power. So my question is: is this war self-
protection or not?

KRISHNAMURTI : I believe that every group that brings about
war always says that it is a self-protective war. There have
always been wars, offensive or defensive; but there are wars
which have been a peculiar, monstrous game throughout the
centuries. And we are, unfortunately, so-called educated and
cultured, yet still we indulge in the most savage forms of
butchery. So could we go into the question of what this deep

73

violence, this aggression in man, is?—could we see whether it is at all possible to be free of it?

There have been those who have said, 'Under no circumstance express violence'; that implies leading a peaceful life although surrounded by people who are very aggressive, violent; it implies a kind of nucleus in the midst of people who are savage, brutal, violent. But how does the mind free itself of its accumulated violence, cultured violence, self-protective violence, the violence of aggression, the violence of competition, the violence of trying to be somebody, the violence of trying to discipline oneself according to a pattern, trying to become somebody, trying to suppress and bully oneself, brutalise oneself, in order to be non-violent—how is the mind to be free of all such forms of violence?

There are so many different kinds of violence. Shall we go into each kind of violence or shall we take the whole structure of violence? Can we look at the whole spectrum of violence, not just at one part of it?

The source of violence is the 'me', the ego, the self, which expresses itself in so many ways—in division, in trying to become or be somebody—which divides itself as the 'me' and the 'not me', as the unconscious and the conscious; the 'me' that identifies with the family or not with the family, with the community or not with the community and so on. It is like a stone dropped in a lake : the waves spread and spread, at the centre is the 'me'. As long as the 'me' survives in any form, very subtly or grossly, there must be violence.

But to ask the question, 'What is the root cause of violence?', to try to find out what the cause is, is not necessarily to get rid of it.

I think, if I were to know why I am brutal, that I would have finished with it. Then I spend weeks, months, years, searching for the cause, or reading the explanations given by experts, of the various causes of violence or aggression; but in the end I am still violent. So, do we enquire into this question of violence through the discovery of the cause and the effect?

74

—or do we take the whole and look at it? We see that the cause becomes the effect and the effect becomes the cause—there is no cause and no effect so markedly different—it is a chain, a cause becoming the effect and the effect becoming the cause—and we go along this process indefinitely. But if we could look at this whole problem of violence, we will comprehend it so vitally that it will come to an end.

We have built a society which is violent and we, as human beings, are violent; the environment, the culture in which we live, is the product of our endeavour, of our struggle, of our pain, of our appalling brutalities. So the most important question is : is it possible to end this tremendous violence in oneself? That is really the question.

Questioner: Is it possible to transform violence?

KRISHNAMURTI : Violence is a form of energy; it is energy utilised in a certain way which becomes aggression. But we are not for the moment trying to transform or change violence but to understand it and comprehend it so fully that one is free of it; the mind has gone beyond it—whether it has transcended it or transformed it, is not so relevant. Is it possible?—is it not possible?—it is possible—these words! How does one think about violence? How does one look at violence? Please listen to the question : how does one know that one is violent? When one is violent, is one aware that one is violent? How does one know violence? This question of knowing is really complex. When I say, 'I know you', what does 'I know' mean? I know you as you were when I met you yesterday, or ten years ago. But between ten years ago and now you have changed and I have changed, therefore I do not know you. I know you only as of the past, therefore I can never say 'I know you'—do please understand this simple thing first. Therefore I can only say, 'I've been violent, but I do not know what violence is now.' You say something to me which irritates my nerves and I am angry. A second later, you say, 'I've been angry.' At the moment of anger you do not recognise it, only later do you do that. You have to examine the structure of recognition; if you do not understand that you will not be able to meet anger afresh. I am angry, but I realise I am angry a moment later. The realisation is the recognition that I have been angry; it is taking place after I have been angry—otherwise I do not know it as anger. See what has happened : the recognition interferes with the actuality. I am always translating the present actuality in terms of the past.

So can one, without translating the present in terms of the past, look at the response anew, with a fresh mind? You call me a fool and my whole blood comes to the surface and says, 'You're another.' And what has taken place, in me, emotionally, inwardly? I have an image about myself as something which I think is desirable, noble, worthwhile; and you are insulting that image. It is that image that responds, which is the old. So the next question is : can the response not be from the old?—can there be an interval between the 'old' and the new actuality?—can the old be hesitant, so as to allow the new to take place? I think that is where the whole problem is.

Questioner: Are you saying that all violence is just the division between what is not and what is?

KRISHNAMURTI : No, sir. Let us begin again. We are violent. Throughout existence, human beings have been violent and are violent. I want to find out, as a human being, how to transcend this violence, how to go beyond it. What am I to do? I see what violence has done in the world, how it has destroyed every form of relationship, how it has brought deep agony in oneself, misery—I see all that. And I say to myself, I want to live a really peaceful life in which there is deep abundance of love—all the violence must go. Now what have I to do? First I must not escape from it; let us be sure of that. I must not escape from the fact that I am violent— 'escaping' being condemning it or justifying it, or the naming of it as violence—the naming is a form of condemnation, a form of justification.

I have to realise that the mind must not be distracted from this fact of violence, neither in seeking the cause nor in the explanation of the cause, nor in naming the fact that I am violent, nor in justifying it, condemning it, trying to get rid of it. These are all forms of distraction from the fact of violence. The mind must be absolutely clear that there is no escape from it; nor must there be the exercise of will which says, 'I will conquer it'—will is the very essence of violence.

Questioner: Basically, are we trying to find what violence is by finding the order in it?

KRISHNAMURTI : No, sir. How can there be order in violence? —violence is disorder.

There must be no escape from it of any kind, no intellectual or explanatory justification—see the difficulty of this, for the mind is so cunning, so sharp to escape, because it does not know what to do with its violence. It is not capable of dealing with it—or it thinks it is not capable—therefore it escapes. Every form of escape, distraction, of movement away, sustains violence. If one realises this, then the mind is confronted with the fact of 'what is' and nothing else.

Questioner: How can you tell whether it is violence if you do not name it?

KRISHNAMURTI : When you name it you are relating it through the name to the past, therefore you are looking at it

77

with the eyes that are touched by the past, therefore you are not looking at it afresh—that is all. Do you get the point?

You look at violence, justifying it, saying that the violence is necessary in order to live in this monstrous society, saying that violence is part of nature—'look, nature kills'—you are conditioned to look with condemnation, justification or resistance. You can only look at it afresh, anew, when you become aware that you are identifying what you see with the images of what you already know and that therefore you are not looking at it afresh. So the question then arises: how are these images formed, what is the mechanism that forms images? My wife says to me, 'You are a fool.' I do not like it and it leaves a mark on my mind. She says something else; that also leaves a mark on my mind. These marks are the images of memory. Now when she says to me, 'You are a fool', if at that very minute I am aware, giving attention, then there is no marking at all—she may be right.

So inattention breeds images; attention frees the mind from the image. This is very simple. In the same way, if when I am angry I become completely attentive, then there is not that inattention which allows the past to come in and interfere with the actual perception of anger at the moment.

Questioner: Is that not an act of will?

KRISHNAMURTI: We said: 'Will is in essence violence.' Let us examine what will is: 'I want to do that'—'I won't have that'—'I shall do that'—I resist, I demand, I desire, which are forms of resistance. When you say, 'I will that', it is a form of resistance and resistance is violence.

Questioner: I follow you when you say that we avoid the problem by seeking an answer; that gets away from 'what is'.

KRISHNAMURTI: So, I want to know how to look at 'what is'.

Now, we are trying to find out if it is possible to transcend violence. We were saying: 'Do not escape from it; do not move away from that central fact of violence.' The question was asked: 'How do you know it is violence?'—do you know it only because you are able to recognise it as having been violence? But when you look at it without naming, without justifying or condemning (which are all the conditioning of the past) then you are looking at it afresh—are you not? Then is it violence? This is one of the most difficult things to do, because all our living is conditioned by the past. Do you know what it is to live in the present?

Questioner: You say, 'Be free of violence'—that includes a lot more; how far does freedom go?

KRISHNAMURTI: Go into freedom; what does it mean? There are all the deep-down angers, frustrations, resistances; the mind must also be free of those, must it not? I am asking: can the mind be free of active violence in the present, be free of all the unconscious accumulations of hate, anger, bitterness, which are there, deep down? How is this to be done?

Questioner: If one is free of this violence in oneself, then when one sees violence outside of oneself, is one not depressed? What is one to do?

KRISHNAMURTI: What one is to do is to teach another. Teaching another is the highest profession in the world—not for money, not for your big bank account, but just to teach, to tell others.

Questioner: What is the easiest way to . . .

KRISHNAMURTI: What is the easiest way? . . . (*Laughter.*)
. . . A circus! Sir, you teach another and by teaching you are
learning yourself. It is not that first you have learnt, accumulated, then you inform. You yourself are violent; understanding yourself is to help another to understand himself, therefore the teaching is the learning. You do not see the beauty
of all this.

So, let us go on. Do you not want to know from your heart
what love is? Has it not been the human cry, for millennia, to
find out how to live peacefully, how to have real abundance
of love, compassion. That can only come into being when
there is the real sense of 'non-me', you understand. And we
say : Look, to find that out—whether it is from loneliness, or
anger, or bitterness—look, without any escape. The escape is
the naming of it, so do not name it, look at it. And then see
—not naming—if bitterness exists.

Questioner: Do you advocate getting rid of all violence, or is
some violence healthy in one's life? I do not mean physical
violence, but getting rid of frustrations. Can this be helpful,
trying to keep from being frustrated?

KRISHNAMURTI: No, Madame. The answer is in the
question : Why are we frustrated? Have you ever asked yourself why you are frustrated? And to answer that question
have you ever asked : What is fulfilment?—why do you want
to fulfil? Is there such a thing as fulfilment? What is it that
is fulfilling?—is it the 'me', the 'me' that is violent, the 'me'
that is separating, the 'me' that says, 'I am bigger than you',
that pursues ambition, fame, notoriety? Because it wants to
achieve, it is frustrated when it cannot achieve; it therefore
becomes bitter. Do you see that there is such a thing as the
'me' wanting to expand itself, which, when it cannot expand,

feels frustrated and therefore bitter?—that bitterness, that desire to expand, is violence. Now when you see the truth of that, then there is no desire for fulfilment at all, therefore there is no frustration.

Questioner: Plants and animals are both living things, they both try to survive. Do you draw a distinction between killing animals to eat and killing plants to eat? If so why?

KRISHNAMURTI : One has to survive, so one kills the least sensitive thing that is available. I have never eaten meat in all my life. And I believe some scientists are gradually coming to that point of view also : if they do, then you will all accept it!

Questioner: It seems to me, that everyone here is used to Aristotelian thinking, and you are using non-Aristotelian tactics; and the gap is so complete I am amazed. How can we commune very closely?

KRISHNAMURTI : That is the difficulty, sir. You are used to one particular formula or language, with a certain meaning, and the speaker has not that particular view. So there is a difficulty in communication. We went into that : we said, the word is the not the thing, the description is not the described, the explanation is not the explained. You keep on sticking to the explanation, holding on to the word; that is why there is difficulty.

So : we see what violence is in the world—part of fear, part of pleasure. There is a tremendous drive for excitement; we want that, and we encourage society to give it to us. And then we blame society; whereas it is we who are responsible. And we are asking ourselves whether the terrific energy of this violence can be used differently. To be violent needs energy : can that energy be transformed or moved in another direction? Now, in the very understanding and seeing the truth of that, that energy becomes entirely different.

Questioner: Are you saying then that non-violence is absolute?—that violence is an aberration of what could be?

KRISHNAMURTI: Yes, if you want to put it that way.

We are saying that violence is a form of energy and love is also a form of energy—love without jealousy, without anxiety, without fear, without bitterness, without all the agony that goes with so-called love. Now, violence is energy, and love hedged about, surrounded with jealousy, is also another form of energy. To transcend both, go beyond both, implies the same energy moved in a totally different direction or dimension.

Questioner: Love with jealousy is actually violence?

KRISHNAMURTI: Of course it is.

Questioner: So you have the two energies, you have the violence and the love.

KRISHNAMURTI: It is the same energy, sir.

Questioner: When should we have psychic experiences?

KRISHNAMURTI: What has that to do with violence? When should you have psychic experiences? Never! Do you know what it means to have psychic experiences? To have the experience, extra-sensory perceptive experience, you must be extraordinarily mature, extraordinarily sensitive, and therefore

82

extraordinarily intelligent; and if you are extraordinarily intelligent, you do not want psychic experience. (*Laughter.*)

Do give your heart to this, please: human beings are destroying each other through violence, the husband is destroying the wife and the wife is destroying the husband. Though they sleep together, walk together, each lives in isolation with his own problems, with his own anxieties; and this isolation is violence. Now when you see all this so clearly in front of you—see it, not just think about it—when you see the danger of it, you act, do you not? When you see a dangerous animal, you act; there is no hesitation, there is no argument between you and the animal—you just act, you run away or do something. Here we are arguing because you do not see the tremendous danger of violence.

If you actually, with your heart, see the nature of violence, see the danger of it, you are finished with it. Now how can one point out the danger of it, if you do not want to see?—neither Aristotelian nor non-Aristotelian language will help you.

Questioner: How do we meet violence in other people?

KRISHNAMURTI: That is really quite a different problem, is it not? My neighbour is violent: how shall I deal with it? Turn the other cheek? He is delighted. What shall I do? Would you ask that question if you were really non-violent, if there were no violence in you? Do listen to this question. If in your heart, in your mind, there is no violence at all, no hate, no bitterness, no sense of fulfilment, no wanting to be free, no violence at all, would you ask that question about how you meet the neighbour who is violent? Or would you know then what to do with your neighbour? Others may call what you do violent, but you may not be violent; at the moment your neighbour acts violently you will know how to deal with the situation. But a third person, watching, might say, 'You are also violent'. But you know you are not violent. So what is

important is to be for yourself completely without violence—
and it does not matter what another calls you.

*Questioner: Is not the belief in the unity of all things just as
human as the belief in the division of all things?*

KRISHNAMURTI : Why do you want to believe in anything?
Why do you want to believe in the unity of all human
beings?—we are not united, that is a fact; why do you want
to believe in something which is non-factual. There is this
whole question of belief; just think, you have your belief and
another has his belief; and we fight and kill each other for a
belief.

Why do you have any belief at all? Do you have belief
because you are afraid? No? Do you believe that the sun
rises?—it is there to see, you do not have to believe in that.
Belief is a form of division and therefore of violence. To be
free of violence implies freedom from everything that man has
put to another man, belief, dogma, rituals, my country, your
country, your god and my god, my opinion, your opinion,
my ideal. All those help to divide human beings and therefore
breed violence. And though organised religions have preached
the unity of mankind, each religion thinks it is far superior to
the other.

*Questioner: I interpreted what you were saying about unity
to mean that those who preach unity are actually aiding the
division.*

KRISHNAMURTI : Quite right, sir.

*Questioner: Is the purpose for living just to be able to cope
with existence?*

KRISHNAMURTI : You say, 'Is this the purpose of living?'—
but why do you want a purpose for living?—live. Living is its
own purpose; why do *you* want a purpose? Look : each one
has his own purpose, the religious man his purpose, the
scientist his purpose, the family man his purpose and so on,
all dividing. The life of a man who has a purpose is breeding
violence. It is so clear and simple.

San Diego State College. 8 April 1970.

7

MEDITATION

'If you have this extraordinary thing going in your life, then it is everything; then you become the teacher, the disciple, the neighbour, the beauty of the cloud—you are all that, and that is love.'

WHAT IS MEDITATION? Before we go into that really quite complex and intricate problem we ought to be very clear as to what it is that we are after. We are always seeking something, especially those who are religiously minded; even for the scientist, seeking has become quite an issue—seeking. This factor, of seeking, must be very clearly and definitely understood before we go into what meditation is and why one should meditate at all, what is its use and where does it get you.

The word 'seek'—to run after, to search out—implies, does it not, that we already know, more or less, what we are after. When we say we are seeking truth, or we are seeking God—if we are religiously minded—or we are seeking a perfect life and so on, we must already have in our minds an image or an idea. To find something after seeking it, we must already have known what its contour is, its colour, its substance and so on. Is there not implied in that word, 'seeking', that we have lost something and we are going to find it and that when we find it we shall be able to recognise it—which means that we have already known it, that all we have to do is to go after it and search it out?

In meditation the first thing we realise is that it is no use to seek; for what is sought is predetermined by what you wish; if you are unhappy, lonely, in despair, you will search out hope, companionship, something to sustain you, and you will find it, inevitably.

In meditation, one must lay the foundation, the foundation of order, which is righteousness—not respectability, the social morality which is no morality at all, but the order that comes of understanding disorder : quite a different thing. Disorder must exist as long as there is conflict, both outwardly and inwardly.

Order, which comes of understanding disorder, is not according to a blueprint, according to some authority, or your own particular experience. Obviously this order must come about without effort, because effort distorts—it must come about without any form of control.

We are talking about something very difficult in saying that we must bring about order without control. We must understand disorder, how it comes into being; it is the conflict which is in ourselves. In observing it, it is understood; it is not a matter of overcoming it, throttling it, suppressing it. To observe without any distortion, without any compulsive or directive impulse, is quite an arduous task.

Control implies either suppression, rejection or exclusion; it implies a division between a controller and the thing controlled; it implies conflict. When one understands this, control and choice come totally to an end. All this may seem rather difficult and rather contradictory to everything you have thought about. You may say : how can there be order without control, without the action of will? But, as we have said, control implies division, between the one who controls and the thing that is to be controlled; in this division there is conflict, there is distortion. When you really understand this, then there is the ending of the division between the controller and the controlled and therefore comprehension, understanding. When there is understanding of what actually is, then there is no need for control.

So there are these two essential things that must be completely understood if we are to go into the question of what meditation is : first, there is no use in seeking; second, there must be that order which comes from the understanding of disorder which comes from control, with all the implications of the duality and the contradiction which arises between the observer and the observed.

Order comes when the one who is angry and tries to get rid of anger sees that he is anger itself. Without this understanding you really cannot possibly know what meditation is. Do not fool yourself with all the books written about meditation, or with all the people who tell you how to meditate, or the groups that are formed in order to meditate. For if there is no order, which is virtue, the mind must live in the effort of contradiction. How can such a mind be aware of the whole implication of meditation?

With one's whole being one must come upon this strange thing called love—and therefore be without fear. We mean love that is not touched by pleasure, by desire, by jealousy— love that knows no competition, that does not divide, as my love and your love. Then the mind—including the brain and the emotions—is in complete harmony; and this must be, otherwise meditation becomes self-hypnosis.

You must work very hard, to find out the activities of your own mind, how it functions, with its self-centred activities, the 'me' and the 'not me'; you must be quite familiar with yourself and all the tricks that the mind plays upon itself, the illusions and the delusions, the imagery and the imagining of all the romantic ideas that one has. A mind that is capable of sentimentality is incapable of love; sentiment breeds brutality, cruelty and violence, not love.

To establish this deeply in yourself is quite arduous; it demands a tremendous discipline, to learn by observing what is going on in yourself. That observation is not possible if there is any form of prejudice, conclusion or formula, according to which you are observing. If you are observing according to what a psychologist has said to you, you really are not observing yourself, therefore there is no self-knowing.

You need a mind that is able to stand completely alone—not burdened by the propaganda or the experiences of others. Enlightenment does not come through a leader or through a teacher; it comes through the understanding of what is in yourself—not going away from yourself. The mind has to understand actually what is going on in its own psychological field; it must be aware of what is going on without any distortion, without any choice, without any resentment, bitterness, explanation or justification—it must just be aware.

This basis is laid happily, not compulsively, but with ease, with felicity, without any hope of reaching anything. If you have hope, you are moving away from despair; one has to understand despair, not search out hope. In the understanding of 'what is' there is neither despair nor hope.

Is all this asking too much of the human mind? Unless one asks what may appear to be impossible, one falls into the trap, the limitation, of what is thought to be possible. To fall into this trap is very easy. One has to ask the utmost of the mind and the heart, otherwise one will remain in the convenient and the comfortable possible.

Now are we together still? Verbally, probably we are; but the word is not the thing; what we have done is to describe, and the description is not the described. If you are taking a journey with the speaker you are taking the journey actually, not theoretically, not as an idea but as something that you yourself are actually observing—not something you are experiencing; there is a difference between observation and experience.

There is a vast difference between observation and experience. In observation there is no 'observer' at all, there is only observing; there is not the one who observes and is divided off from the thing observed. Observation is entirely different from the exploration in which analysis is involved. In analysis there is always the 'analyser' and the thing to be analysed. In exploring there is always an entity who explores. In observation there is a continuous learning, not a continuous accumulation. I hope you see the difference. Such learning is different from learning in order to accumulate so that from that accumulation one thinks and acts. An enquiry may be logical, sane and rational, but to observe without the 'observer' is entirely different.

Then there is the question of experience. Why do we want experience? Have you ever thought about it? We have experience all the time, of which we are either cognisant or ignorant. And we want deeper, wider, experiences—mystical, profound, transcendental, godly, spiritual—why? Is it not because one's life is so shoddy, so miserable, so small and petty? One wants to forget all that and move into another dimension altogether. How can a petty mind, worried, fearful, occupied with problem after problem, experience anything other than its own projection and activity? This demand for greater experience is the escaping from that which actually is; yet it is only through that actuality that the most mysterious thing in life is come upon. In experience is involved the process of recognition. When you recognise something, it means you have already known it. Experience, generally, is out of the past, there is nothing new in it. So there is a difference between observation and the craving for experience.

If all this, that is so extraordinarily subtle, demanding great inward attention, is clear, then we can come to our original question: what is meditation? So much has been said about meditation; so many volumes have been written; there are great (I do not know if they are great) yogis who come and teach you how to meditate. The whole of Asia talks about meditation; it is one of their habits, as it is a habit to believe in God or something else. They sit for ten minutes a day in a quiet room and 'meditate', concentrate, fix their mind on an image, an image created by themselves, or by somebody else who has offered that image through propaganda. During those ten minutes they try to control the mind; the mind wants to go back and forth and they battle with it—that game they play everlastingly; and that is what they call meditation.

If one does not know anything about meditation, then one has to find out what it is, actually—not according to anybody —and that may lead one to nothing or it may lead one to everything. One must enquire, ask that question, without any expectation.

To observe the mind—this mind that chatters, that projects ideas, that lives in contradiction, in constant conflict and comparison—I must obviously be very quiet. If I am to listen to what you are saying I must give attention, I cannot be chattering, I cannot be thinking about something else, I must not compare what you are saying with what I already know, I must listen to you completely; the mind must be attentive, must be silent, quiet.

It is imperative to see clearly the whole structure of violence; looking at violence the mind becomes completely still—you do not have to 'cultivate' a still mind. To cultivate a still mind implies the one who cultivates, in the field of time, that which he hopes to achieve. See the difficulty. Those who try to teach meditation, say, 'Control your mind, make your mind absolutely quiet'. You try to control it and everlastingly battle with it; you spend forty years controlling it. The mind that observes does not control and everlastingly battle.

The very act of seeing or listening is attention; this you do not have to practise at all; if you practise, you immediately become inattentive. You are attentive and your mind wanders off; let it wander off, but know that it is inattentive; that awareness of that inattention is attention. Do not battle with inattention; do not try, saying, 'I must be attentive'—it is childish. Know that you are inattentive; be aware, choice-lessly, that you are inattentive—what of it?—and at the moment, in that inattention, when there is action, be aware of that action. Do you understand this? It is so simple. If you do it, it becomes so clear, clear as the waters.

The silence of the mind is beauty in itself. To listen to a bird, to the voice of a human being, to the politician, to the priest, to all the noise of propaganda that goes on, to listen completely silently, is to hear much more, to see much more. Such silence is not possible if your body is not also completely still. The organism, with all its nervous responses—the fidgeting, the ceaseless movement of fingers, the eyes—with all its general restlessness, must be completely still. Have you ever tried sitting completely still without a single movement of the body, including the eyes? Do it for two minutes. In those two minutes the whole thing is revealed—if you know how to look.

The body being still, the flow of blood to the head becomes more. But if you sit crouched and sloppy, then it is more difficult for the blood to go to the head—you must know all this. But, on the other hand, you can do anything and meditate; when in the bus, or when you are driving—it is the most extraordinary thing, that you can meditate while you are driving—be careful, I mean this. The body has its own intelligence, which thought has destroyed. Thought seeks pleasure, and in this way thought leads to indulgence, over-eating, indulging sexually; it compels the body to do certain things—if it is lazy, it forces it not to be lazy, or it suggests taking a pill to keep awake. That way the innate intelligence of the organism is destroyed and it becomes insensitive. One needs great sensitivity, therefore one has to watch what one eats—if one overeats, one knows what happens. When there is great sensitivity, there is intelligence and therefore love; love then is joy and timeless.

Most of us have physical pain, in some form or another. That pain generally disturbs the mind which spends days, even years, thinking about it—'I wish I did not have it'; 'Shall I ever be without it?' When the body has pain, watch it, observe it, do not let thought interfere with it.

The mind, including the brain and the heart, must be in total harmony. Now, what is the point of all this, this kind of life, this kind of harmony, what good is it in this world, where there is so much suffering? If one or two people have this ecstatic life, what is the point of it? What is the point of asking this question?—it has none whatsoever. If you do have this extraordinary thing going in your life, then it is everything; then you become the teacher, the disciple, the neighbour, the beauty of the cloud—you are all that, and that is love.

Then comes another factor in meditation. The waking mind, the mind that is functioning during the day along the lines in which it has been trained, the conscious mind with all its daily activities, continues those activities during sleep in dreams. In dreams there is action going on, of some kind or other, some happening, so that your sleep is a continuation of the waking hours. And there is a lot of mysterious hocus-pocus about dreams—that they need to be interpreted, hence all the professionals interpreting dreams—which you can observe yourself very simply, if you watch your own life during the daytime. Yet why should there be dreams at all? (Though the psychologists say that you must have dreams, otherwise you will go insane.) But when you have observed very closely your waking hours, all your self-centred activities, the fearful, the anxious, the guilty, when you are attentive to that all day then you will see that when you sleep, you have no dreams. The mind has been watching every moment of thought, attentive to its every word; if you do it, you will see the beauty of it—not the tired boredom of watching, but the beauty of watching; you will see then that there is attention in sleep. And meditation, the thing that we have talked about during this hour, becomes extraordinarily important and worthwhile, full of dignity and grace and beauty. When you understand what attention is, not only during waking hours but also during sleep, then the whole of the mind is totally awake. Beyond that, every form of description is not the described; you do not talk about it. All that one can do is point to the door. And if you are willing to go, take a journey to that door, then it is for you to walk beyond; nobody can describe the thing that is not nameable, whether that nameable is nothing or everything—it does not matter. Anybody who describes it does not know. And one who says he knows, does not know.

Questioner: What is quietness, what is silence? Is it the ending of noise?

KRISHNAMURTI: Sound is a strange thing. I do not know if you ever listen to sound—not to sounds which you like or do not like—but just to listen to a sound! Sound in space has an extraordinary effect. Have you ever listened to a jet plane that is passing overhead?—have you, to the deep sound of it, without any resistance? Have you listened and moved with that sound? It has a certain resonance.

Now, what is silence?—is it the 'space' you produce, which you call silence, by control, by suppressing noise? The brain is all the time active, responding to stimuli with its own noise. So what is silence? You understand the question now? Is silence the cessation of that self-created noise?—is it the cessation of chattering, of verbalisation, of every thought? Even when there is no more verbalisation and thought seemingly comes to an end, the brain is still going on. Is not silence therefore not only the end of noise but the complete cessation of all movement? Observe it, go into it, see how your brain, which is the result of millions of years of conditioning, is responding to every stimulus instantly; see whether those brain cells, everlastingly active, chattering, responding, can be still.

Can the mind, the brain, the whole organism, this total psychosomatic thing, be completely still?—not forced, not compelled, not driven, not out of greed saying 'I must be still in order to have the most marvellous experience'? Go into it, find out and see whether your silence is a mere product, or whether it is perhaps because you have laid the foundation. If you have not laid the foundation, which is love, which is virtue, which is goodness, which is beauty, which is real compassion in the depth of your whole being, if you have not done that, your silence is only the ending of noise.

Then there is the whole problem of drugs. In India, in ancient times, there used to be a substance called 'soma'. It was a kind of mushroom of which they drank the juice which produced either tranquillity or all kinds of hallucinatory experiences; those experiences being the result of conditioning. (All experiences are the result of conditioning; if you believe in God, obviously you have the experience of God; but that belief is based on fear and all the agony of conflict; your god is the result of your own fear. And so the most marvellous experience of God is nothing but your own projection.) But they lost the secret of that mushroom, that particular thing called soma. Since then, in India, as here, there are various drugs, hashish, L.S.D., marihuana, you know the multiplicity of them all, tobacco, drink, heroin. Also there is fasting. If you fast, certain chemical actions take place producing a certain clarity and there is delight in that.

If one can live a beautiful life without taking drugs, why take them? But those who have taken them tell us that certain changes take place; a certain vitality, an energy arises and the space between the observer and the observed disappears; things are seen much more clearly. One drug taker says he takes them when he goes to a museum, for then he sees colours more brilliantly then ever before. But you can see those colours in such brilliance without the drug when you pay complete attention, when you observe without the space between you the observer and the thing observed. When you take drugs you depend on them, and sooner or later they have all kinds of disastrous effects.

So there it is—fasting, drugs, which it is hoped will satisfy the desire for great experience, which will produce everything that you want. And what is wanted is such a tawdry affair;

some petty little experience, which is blown up into something extraordinary. So a wise man, a man who has observed all this, puts aside all the stimulants; he observes himself and knows himself. The knowing of himself is the beginning of wisdom and the ending of sorrow.

Questioner: In right relationship, do we really help others? Is it sufficient to love them?

KRISHNAMURTI : What is relationship? What do we mean by relationship? Are we related to anybody?—except sanguinary relationship. What do we mean by that word 'relationship'? Are we ever related to anything when each one of us lives a life of isolation—isolation in the sense of self-centred activity, each with his own problems, his own fears, his own despairs, his desire to fulfil—all enclosing properties. If he is, so-called, related to his wife, he has added images. It is these images that have relationship, and that relationship is called love! Relationship exists only when the image, the isolating process, comes to an end, when you have no ambition for her and she has no ambition for you, when she does not possess you or you possess her, or you depend on her or she on you.

When there is love you will not ask whether it helps or not. A wayside flower, with its beauty, with its perfume, is not asking you who are passing by to come and smell it, to look at it, to enjoy it, to see the beauty, the delicacy, the perishable nature of it—it is there for you to look or not to look. But if you say 'I want to help another', that is the beginning of fear, the beginning of mischief.

San Diego State College. 9 April 1970.

PART III

8

CONTROL AND ORDER

'The very process of control breeds disorder; just as the opposite—lack of control—also breeds disorder.'

THERE ARE SO many frightening things happening in the world; there is so much confusion, violence and brutality. What can one do, as a human being, in a world that is torn apart, in a world where there is so much despair and sorrow? And in oneself there is so much confusion and conflict. What is the relationship of a human being with this corrupt society, where the individual himself is corrupt? What is the way of life in which one can find some kind of peace, some kind of order and yet live in this society which is corrupt, disintegrating? I am sure you must have asked these questions of yourself; and if one has found the right answer, which is extremely difficult, perhaps one can bring about some kind of order in one's life.

What value has one individual who leads an orderly, sane, whole, balanced life in a world that is destroying itself, a world that is constantly threatened by war? What value has individual change? How will it affect this whole mass of human existence? I am sure you have asked these questions. But I think they are wrong questions, because one does not live and act rightly for the sake of somebody else, for the benefit of society. So one must find out, it seems to me, what order is, so as not to be dependent on circumstance, on a particular culture—economic, social or otherwise—because if one does not find out for oneself what order is and the way to live without conflict, one's life is wasted, it has no meaning. As we are living now in constant travail and conflict, life has very little meaning; it actually has no significance at all. Having a little money, going to the office, being conditioned, repeating what others say, having very strong, obstinate opinions and dogmatic beliefs—all such activity has very little meaning. And since it has no meaning, the intellectuals throughout the world try to give it a meaning. If they are religious they give it a particular slant; if they are materialistic they give it another, with a particular philosophy or theory.

So it seems very important—not only now but at all times, if one is at all serious—to find a way of life for oneself, not as a theory, but actually in daily life, a way to live without conflict of any kind at every level of one's being. To find that out one must be serious. These meetings here are not a philosophical or religious entertainment. We are here—if we are serious, and I hope we are—to find out together a way of life not according to any particular formula or theory or principle or belief. Communication implies sharing together, creating together, working together, not merely listening to a lot of words and ideas; we are not dealing with ideas at all. So from the beginning it must be very clear that we are seriously giving our mind and heart to find out if man—if you—can live completely at peace, ending all conflict in all relationships.

To find out, one must look at oneself not according to a particular philosophy or a particular system of thought, or from any particular religious point of view. I think one has to discard all that completely, so that one's mind is free to observe itself in relation to society, in relation to ourselves, to our families, to our neighbour; for only then, in the observation of what is actually going on, is there a possibility of going beyond it. And I hope that is what we are going to do during these talks.

We are not professing a new theory, a new philosophy, nor bringing a religious revelation. There is no teacher, no saviour, no master, no authority—I really mean this—because if you are going to share in what is being said, you must also put aside totally every form of authoritarian, hierarchical outlook; the mind must be free to observe. And it cannot possibly observe if you are following some system, some guide, some principle, or are tethered to any form of belief. The mind must be capable of observing. That is going to be our difficulty, because for most of us knowledge has become a dead weight, a heavy stone round our necks; it has become our habit, our conditioning. The mind that is serious must be free to observe; it must be free of this dead weight which is knowledge, experience, tradition—which is accumulated memory, the past.

So to observe actually 'what is', to see the whole significance of 'what is', the mind must be fresh, clear, undivided. And that is going to be another problem : how to look without this division—the 'me' and the 'not me', and 'we' and 'they'.

As we said, you are observing yourself, watching yourself through the words of the speaker. So the question is : how are you to observe? I do not know if you have ever gone into that question at all. How do you look, hear, observe?—not only yourself, but the sky, the trees, the birds, your neighbour, the politician. How do you listen and observe another, how do you observe yourself? The key to this observation lies in seeing things without division. And can that ever happen? All our existence is fragmented. We are divided in ourselves, we are contradictory. We live in fragmentation—which is an actual fact. One fragment of these many fragments thinks it has the capacity to observe. Although through many associations it has assumed authority, it is still a fragment of the many fragments. And that one fragment looks and says, 'I understand; I know what right action is.'

So being fragmented, broken up, contradictory, there is conflict between the various fragments. You know this as a fact, if you have observed it. And we come to the conclusion that nothing can be done about it, that nothing can be changed. How can this fragmentation be made whole? We realise that to live a harmonious, orderly, sane, healthy life, this fragmentation, this division between the 'you' and the 'me' must come to an end. But we have concluded that this is not possible—that is the dead weight of 'what is'. So we invent theories, we wait for 'grace' from something divine—whatever you call it—to come and miraculously release us. Unfortunately that does not happen. Or you live in an illusion, invent some myth about the higher self, the Atman. This offers an escape.

We are easily persuaded to escape because we do not know how this fragmentation can be made whole. We are not talking of integration, because that implies that somebody brings about integration—one fragment bringing the other fragments together. I hope you see the difficulty of this, how we are broken up into many fragments, conscious or unconscious. And we try many ways. One of the fashionable ways is to have an analyst to do this for you; or you analyse yourself. Please do follow this carefully : there is the analyser and the thing to be analysed. We have never questioned who the analyser is. He is obviously one of the many fragments and he proceeds to analyse the whole structure of oneself. But the analyser himself, being a fragment, is conditioned. When he analyses there are several things involved. First of all, every analysis must be complete or otherwise it becomes the stone round the neck of the analyser when he begins to analyse the next incident, the next reaction. So the memory of the previous analysis increases the burden. And analysis also implies time; there are so many reactions, associations and memories to be analysed that it will take all your life. By the time you have completely analysed yourself—if that is ever possible—you are ready for the grave.

That is one of our conditionings, the idea that we must analyse ourselves, look at ourselves introspectively. In this analysis there is always the censor, the one who controls, guides, shapes; there is always the conflict between the analyser and the thing to be analysed. So one has to see this—not as a theory, not as something that you have accumulated as knowledge; knowledge is excellent in its own place but not when you are trying to understand the whole structure of your being. If you use knowledge through association and accumulation, through analysis, as a means of understanding yourself, then you have stopped learning about yourself. To learn there must be freedom to observe without the censor.

We can see this going on in ourselves, actually, as 'what is', night and day, endlessly. And seeing the truth of it—the truth, not as an opinion—the futility, the mischief, the wastage of energy and time, then the whole process of analysis comes to an end. I hope you are doing this as you are listening to what is being said. Because through analysis there is the continuation of the endless chain of association; therefore one says to oneself, 'One can never change; this conflict, this misery, this confusion is inevitable, this is the way of life.' So one becomes mechanical, violent, brutal, and stupid. When one really observes this as a fact, one sees the truth of it; one can only see this truth when one actually sees what is going on—the 'what is'. Do not condemn it, do not rationalise it—just observe it. And you can only observe when there is no association in your observation.

As long as there is the analyser there must be the censor who brings about this whole problem of control. I do not know if you have ever realised that from the moment we are born till we die, we are always controlling ourselves. The 'must' and the 'must not', the 'should be' and the 'should not'. Control implies conformity, imitation, following a particular principle, an ideal, eventually leading to that appalling thing called respectability. Why should one control at all?—which does not mean you entirely lose all control. One has to understand what is implied in control. The very process of control breeds disorder; just as the opposite—lack of control—also breeds disorder.

One has to explore, understand, look at what is implied in control and see the truth of it; then one lives a life of order in which there is no control whatsoever. Disorder is brought about by this contradiction caused by the censor, the analyser, the entity that has separated himself from the various other fragments, and who is trying to impose what he thinks is right.

So one has to understand this particular form of conditioning, which is : that we are all bound and shaped by control. I do not know if you ever asked yourself why you control anything at all. You do control, don't you? Why? What makes you control? What is the root of this imitation, this conformity? Obviously one of the factors is our conditioning, our culture, our religious and social sanctions, as 'you must do this' and 'not do that'. In this control there is always the will, which is a form of urgent desire that controls, that shapes, that directs. Observe this, please, as you are listening; actually observe it and you will see that something quite different comes about. We control ourselves, our tempers, our desires, our appetites, because it is always safe. There is great security in control, with all its suppressions and contradictions, with all its struggles and conflicts; there is a certain sense of safety. And also it assures us that we shall never fail.

Where there is division between the controller and the thing controlled, there is no goodness. Goodness does not lie in separation. Virtue is a state of mind in which there is no separation, therefore there is no control which involves division. Control implies suppression, contradiction, effort, the demand for security—all in the name of goodness, beauty, virtue; but it is the very denial of virtue, and is therefore disorder.

So can one observe without division, without the observer opposed to the thing to be observed, without the knowledge which the observer has acquired, which separates him when he looks? For the observer is the enemy of the good—though he desires order, though he attempts to bring about righteous behaviour, to live peacefully. The observer who separates himself from the thing observed is the very source of all that is not good. Do you see all this? Or are you just being casually entertained on a Saturday afternoon? Do you know what all this means?—that the mind is no longer analysing but actually observing, seeing directly and therefore acting directly. It means a mind in which there is no division whatsoever; it is a total, whole mind—which means being sane. It is the neurotic who has to control; when he comes to the point of having controlled himself totally, he is completely neurotic so that he cannot move, is not free.

See the truth of this! The truth is not 'what is'—the 'what is' is the division, the Black and White, the Arab and the Jew, all the mess that is going on in this frightful world. Because the mind has divided itself it is not a whole, sane, healthy, holy mind. And because of this division in the mind itself, there is so much corruption, so much disorder, so much violence and brutality. So the question then is : can the mind observe without division, where the observer is the observed? To look at a tree, at a cloud, at the beauty of the lovely spring, to look at yourself, without the burden of knowledge; to look at yourself and learn at the moment of observation, without the accumulation of learning, so that the mind is free all the time to observe. It is only the young mind that learns, not the mind that is burdened with knowledge. And to learn means to observe oneself without division, without analysis, without the censor dividing the good from the bad, the what 'should be' from the 'should not be'. This is one of the most important things, because if you so observe, the mind will discover that all conflict comes to an end. In that there is total goodness. It is only such a mind that can act righteously, and in that there is great joy—not the joy stimulated through pleasure.

I wonder if you would care to ask any questions? You must question everything, including your pet beliefs, your ideals, your authorities, your scriptures, your politicians. Which means there must be a certain quality of scepticism. But scepticism must be kept on the leash; you must let it go when necessary, so that the mind can see freely, run rapidly. When you question, it must be your own particular problem, not a casual, superficial question that will entertain you; it must be something of your own. If this is so, then you will put the right question. And if it is the right question you will have the right answer, because the very act of putting that right question shows you the answer in itself. So one must—if I may point this out—put the right question. Then in putting the right question we can both of us share, partake together, in that problem. Your problem is not different from other people's problems. All problems are interrelated, and if you can understand one problem completely, wholly, you have understood all other problems. Therefore it is very important to put the right question. But even if it is the wrong question, you will find that in putting the wrong question you will also know when to ask the right question. You must do both : then we shall come to putting always the fundamental, real, true question.

Questioner : What is the ultimate reason or purpose of human existence?

KRISHNAMURTI : Do you know any purposes? The way we live has no meaning and no purpose. We can invent a purpose, the purpose of perfection, enlightenment, reaching the highest form of sensitivity; we can invent endless theories. And we are caught in those theories, making them our problems. Our daily life has no meaning, no purpose, except to make a bit of money and lead an idiotic kind of life. One can observe all this, not in theory but actually in oneself; the endless battle in oneself, seeking a purpose, seeking enlightenment, going all over the world—specially to India or to Japan—to learn a technique of meditation. You can invent a thousand purposes, but you need not go anywhere, not to the Himalayas, to a monastery, or to any Ashram—which is another form of concentration camp—because everything is in you. The highest, the immeasurable, is in you, if you know how to look. Do not assume it is there—that is one of the stupid tricks we play upon ourselves, that we are God, that we are the 'perfect' and all the rest of that childish stuff. Yet through the illusion, through 'what is', through the measurable, you find something that is immeasurable; but you must begin with yourself, where you can discover for yourself how to look. That is: to look without the observer

Questioner : Would you please define, in the context of which you were speaking, control in relation to restraint.

KRISHNAMURTI : One has to understand the full meaning of that word control, not only according to the dictionary, but how the mind has been conditioned to control—control being suppression. In that there is the censor, the controller, the division, the conflict, the restraining, the holding, the inhibiting. When one is aware of all this, the mind then becomes very sensitive and therefore highly intelligent. We have destroyed that intelligence, which is also in the body, in the organism; we have perverted it through our pleasurable tastes and appetites. Also the mind has been shaped, controlled, conditioned through centuries by the culture, by fear, by belief. When one realises this, not theoretically but actually, when one is aware of this, then one will find sensitivity responds intelligently without inhibition, control, suppression or restraint. But one has to understand the structure and the nature of control, which has bred so much disorder in ourselves—the will, which is the very centre of contradiction and therefore of control. Look at it, observe it in your life and you will discover all this and more. But when you make your discovery into knowledge, into some dead weight, then you are lost. Because knowledge is the accumulation of associations, an endless chain. And if the mind is caught in that, then change is impossible.

Questioner: Can you explain to me how the mind overcomes the body so that it can levitate?

KRISHNAMURTI: Are you really interested in this? I do not know why you want to levitate. You know, sirs, the mind is always seeking something mysterious, something hidden, which nobody else will discover except yourself, and that gives you a tremendous sense of importance, vanity, prestige—you become the 'Mystic'. But there is real mystery, something really sacred, when you understand the whole of this life, this whole existence. In that there is great beauty, great joy. There is a tremendous thing called the immeasurable. But you must understand the measurable. And the immeasurable is not the opposite of the measurable.

There have been photographs of people who have levitated. The speaker has seen it and other forms of unimportant things. If you are really interested in levitation—I do not know why you should be, but if you are—you have to have a marvellous, highly sensitive body; you must not drink, nor smoke, nor take drugs, nor eat meat. You must have a body that is utterly pliable, healthy, that has its own intelligence, not the intelligence imposed by the mind on the body. And if you have gone through all that, then you may find that levitation has no worth in it!

London. 16 May 1970.

9

TRUTH

'Truth is not "what is", but the understanding of "what is" opens the door to truth.'

THERE ARE SEVERAL things we should talk about, such as education, the significance of dreams, and whether it is at all possible, living in a world that has become so mechanical and imitative, for the mind ever to be free. We may approach the problem by going into the question of whether the mind can be free from all sense of conformity. We have to deal with the whole problem of existence, not one part of it, not only the technical side of life and the earning of a livelihood, but also we have to consider this whole question of how to transform society; whether this is possible through revolt, or if there is a different kind of inward revolution which will inevitably bring about a different kind of society. I think we should go into that and then come upon the question of meditation. Because—if you will forgive me for saying so—I do not think you know what is implied in meditation. Most of us have read about it or have been told what it is and we have tried to practise it. What the speaker has to say about meditation may be quite contrary to all that you know or practise or have experienced. One cannot search for truth; therefore one must understand the meaning of seeking. So it is a very complex question; meditation requires the highest form of sensitivity, a tremendous quality of silence, not induced, not disciplined, not cultivated. And that can only be, or come about, when we understand, psychologically, how to live, because our life as we live it daily, is in conflict; it is a series of conformities, controls, suppressions, and the revolt against all that.

There is the whole question of how to live a life without violence of any kind; for without really understanding and being free from violence, meditation is not possible. You can play with it, go to the Himalayas to learn how to breathe and sit properly, do a little bit of yoga and think you have learnt meditation, but that is all rather childish. To come upon that extraordinary thing called meditation, the mind must be completely free of all sense of violence. Therefore it may be worthwhile to talk about violence and see if the mind can actually be free of that; not go off romantically into some kind of stupor called meditation.

Volumes have been written as to why man is aggressive. Anthropologists give explanations and each expert puts it in his own way, contradicting or enlarging on what most of us know rationally : that human beings are violent. We think violence is merely a physical act, going to war and killing others. We have accepted war as the way of life. And accepting it, we do nothing about it. Casually or devotedly we may become pacifists in one part of our own life, but for the rest we are in conflict; we are ambitious, we are competitive, we make tremendous efforts; such effort implies conflict and therefore violence. Any form of conformity, any form of distortion —purposely or unconsciously—is violence. To discipline oneself according to a pattern, an ideal, a principle, is a form of violence. Any distortion, without understanding actually 'what is' and going beyond it, is a form of violence. And yet, is it at all possible to end violence in oneself without any conflict, any opposition?

We are used to a society, a morality, that is based on violence. We all know this. From childhood we are brought up to be violent, to imitate, to conform—consciously or unconsciously. We do not know how to get out of it. We say to ourselves it is impossible, man must be violent, but violence can be done with gloves on, politely and so on. So we must go into this question of violence, because without understanding violence and fear, how can there be love? Can the mind which has accepted conformity to a society, to a principle, to a social morality which is not moral at all, a mind that has been conditioned by religions to believe—accepting the idea of God, or rejecting it—can it free itself without any form of struggle, without any resistance? Violence begets more violence; resistance only creates other forms of distortion.

Without reading books or listening to professors or 'saints', one can observe one's own mind. After all, that is the beginning of self-knowledge : to know oneself, not according to some psychologist or analyst, but by observing oneself. One can see how heavily the mind is conditioned—there is nationalism, racial and class differences, and all the rest of it. If one is aware of it one becomes conscious of this conditioning, this vast propaganda in the name of God, in the name of Communism or what you will, which has shaped us from childhood, during centuries upon centuries. Becoming aware of it, can the mind uncondition itself, free itself from all sense of conformity and therefore have freedom?

How is this to be done? How can I, or you, become aware, knowing one's mind is solidly conditioned not only superficially but deep down? How is this conditioning to be broken down? If this is not possible we shall live everlastingly in conformity—even if there is a new pattern, a new structure of society or a new set of beliefs, new dogmas and new propagandas, it is still conformity. And if there is to be any kind of social change, there must be a different kind of education—so that children are not brought up to conform.

So there is this question : how is the mind to free itself from conditioning? I do not know if you have ever tried it, gone into it very deeply, not only at the conscious level but at the deeper layers of consciousness. Actually, is there a division between the two? Or is it one movement, in which we are only conscious of the superficial movement which has been educated to conform to the demands of a particular society or culture?

As we said the other day : we are not merely listening to a few sets of words, because that has no value at all. But by partaking in what is being said, sharing it, working together, you will find out for yourself how to observe this total movement, without separation, without division; because wherever there is any kind of division—racial, intellectual, emotional, or the division of the opposites, the 'me' and the 'not me', the higher self and the lower self and so on—it must inevitably bring about conflict. Conflict is a waste of energy and to understand all that we are discussing you need a great deal of energy.

The mind being so conditioned, how can it observe itself, without division into the observer and the thing observed? The space between the observer and the observed, the distance, the time-interval, is a contradiction and the very essence of division. Therefore when the observer separates himself from the thing observed, he not only acts as a censor but brings about this duality and hence conflict.

So can the mind observe itself without the division of the observer and the observed? Do you understand the problem? When you observe that you are jealous, envious—which is a very common factor—and are aware of it, there is always the observer who says 'I must not be jealous.' Or the observer gives a reason for being jealous, justifying it—is that not so? There is the observer and the thing observed; the former observes jealousy as something separate from himself which he tries to control, which he tries to get rid of; hence there is a conflict between the observer and the thing observed. The observer is one of the many fragments which we are.

Are we communicating with each other? Do you understand what we mean by communicating? It is sharing together, not just understanding verbally, intellectually seeing the point. There is no intellectual understanding of *anything*; especially when we are concerned with great fundamental human problems.

So when you really understand the truth, that division of any kind must inevitably breed conflict, you will see that it is a waste of energy and therefore causes distortion and violence and everything else that follows from conflict. When you really understand this—not verbally but actually—then you will see how to observe without the time-interval and the space between the observer and the thing observed; you will see how to observe the conditioning, the violence, the oppression, the brutality, the appalling things that are going on in the world and in oneself. Are you doing it as we are talking? Do not say 'yes' because it is one of the most difficult things, to observe without the observer, without the verbaliser, without the entity that is full of knowledge which is the past, without that space between the observer and the thing observed. Do it —observe a tree, a cloud, the beauty of the spring, the new leaf—and you will see what an extraordinary thing it is. But then you will see that you have never seen the tree before, never!

When you observe, you are always observing with an image or through an image. You have an image, as knowledge, when you look at the tree or when you look at your wife or husband; you have the image of what she is or what he is, which has been built up for twenty, thirty or forty years. So one image looks at another image and these images have their own relationships; therefore there is no actual relationship. Do recognise this very simple fact, that we look at almost everything in life with an image, with a prejudice, with a preconceived idea. We never look with fresh eyes; our mind is never young.

So we must observe ourselves—who are part of violence— and the immense search for pleasure with its fears, with its frustrations, with the agony of loneliness, the lack of love, the despair. To observe this whole structure of oneself without the observer, to see it as it is without any distortion, without any judgment, condemnation or comparison—which are all the movement of the observer, of the 'me' and the 'not-me'—demands the highest form of discipline. We are using the word 'discipline' not in the sense of conformity or coercion—not as discipline brought about through reward and punishment. To observe anything—your wife, your neighbour or a cloud—one must have a mind that is very sensitive; this very observation brings about its own discipline, which is non-conformity. Therefore the highest form of discipline is no discipline.

So to observe the thing called violence without division, without the observer, to see the conditioning, the structure of belief, the opinions, the prejudices, is to see what you are; that is 'what is'. When you observe it and there is a division, then you say, 'It is impossible to change.' Man has lived like this for millennia and you go on living in this way. Saying 'It is not possible' deprives one of energy. Only when you see what is possible in the highest form, then you have plenty of energy.

So one has to observe actually 'what is', not the image you have about 'what is', but what you actually are; never saying 'it is ugly' or 'beautiful'. You know what you are only through comparison. You say, 'I am dull' compared to somebody who is very intelligent, very alive. Have you ever tried to live a life without comparing yourself with anybody or anything? What then are you? Then, what you are is 'what is'. Then you can go beyond it, find out what truth is! So this whole question of freeing the mind from conditioning lies in how the mind observes.

I do not know if you have ever gone into the question of what love is, or have thought about it or enquired into it. Is love pleasure? Is love desire? Is love something to be cultivated, a thing made respectable by society? If it is pleasure, as it apparently is, from everything that one has observed—not only sexual pleasure but the moral pleasure, the pleasure of achievement, of success, the pleasure of becoming, of being somebody, implying competitiveness and conformity—is that love? An ambitious man, even the man who says, 'I must find truth', who pursues what he considers to be truth, can he know what love is?

Should we not intelligently enquire into this?—that is, seeing what it is not; through negation come to the positive. Denying what love is not. Jealousy is not love; the memory of a pleasure, sexual or otherwise, is not love; the cultivation of virtue, the constant effort of trying to be noble, is not love. And when you say, 'I love you', what does it mean? The image you have about him or her, the sexual pleasures and all the rest of it, the comfort, the companionship, never being alone and frightened to be alone, always wanting to be loved, to possess, to be possessed, to dominate, to assert, to be aggressive—is all that love? If you see the absurdity of it, not verbally but actually as it is, all the nonsense that one talks about love—love of one's country, love of God—when you see all the sensuality of it—we are not condemning sex, we are observing it—when you actually observe it as it is, you see that your love of God is love out of fear, your week-end religion is fear. And to observe it totally, implies no division. Where there is no division there is goodness; you do not have to cultivate goodness. So can the mind—the mind including the brain, the whole structure—totally observe the thing that it calls love, with all its mischief, with all its pettiness and its bourgeois mediocrity? To observe that, there must be the denial of everything that love is not.

You know, there is a great difference between joy and pleasure. You can cultivate pleasure, think about it a great deal and have more of it. You had pleasure yesterday and you can think about it, chew on it and you will want it repeated tomorrow. In pleasure there is a motive in which there is possessiveness, domination, conformity and all the rest of it. There is great pleasure in conformity—Hitler, Mussolini, Stalin and so on, made people conform, because there is great security and safety in it. So when you see all that, when you are free of it—actually, not verbally, never to be jealous, never to dominate or be possessed—when the mind has swept away all that, then you know what love is—you do not have to seek it.

When the mind has understood the meaning of the word love, then you are bound to ask: what is death? Because love and death go together. If the mind does not know how to die to the past, it does not know what love is. Love is not of time, it is not a thing to be remembered—you cannot remember joy and cultivate it; it comes uninvited.

So what is death? I do not know if you have observed death, not someone dying, but yourself dying. It is one of the most difficult things, not to identify yourself with something. Most of us identify ourselves with our furniture, with our house, with our wife or husband, with our government, with our country, with the image that we have about ourselves, identifying with something greater—the greater may be a greater tribalism, which is the nation; or you identify yourself with a particular quality or image. Not to identify with your furniture, with your knowledge, with your experiences, with your techniques and your technological knowledge as a scientist or engineer, to end all identification, is a form of death. Do it sometime and you will find out what it means: not bitterness, not hopelessness, not a sense of despair, but an extraordinary feeling—a mind that is completely free to observe and therefore live.

Unfortunately we have divided life and death. What we are frightened of is 'not to live'—this 'living' which we call life. And when you actually examine what this living is, not theoretically, but observe it with your eyes and your ears, with everything you have, you see how shoddy it is, how small, petty, shallow; you may have a Rolls-Royce, a big house, a lovely garden, a title, a degree, but inwardly life is an everlasting battle, a constant struggle, with contradictions, opposing desires, multiple wants.

That is what we call living and to that we cling. Anything

that puts an end to that—unless you are tremendously identified with your body—we call death; though the physical organism ends too. And being afraid of ending, we have all kinds of beliefs. They are all escapes—including re-incarnation. What matters is how you live now, not what you will be in the next life. Then the question is whether the mind can live entirely without time. One must really understand this question of the past—the past as yesterday, through today, shaping tomorrow from what has been yesterday. Can that mind—which is the result of time, of evolution—be free of the past? —which is to die. It is only a mind that knows this, that can come upon this thing called meditation. Without understanding all this, to try to meditate is just childish imagination.

Truth is not 'what is', but the understanding of 'what is' opens the door to truth. If you do not actually understand 'what is', what you are, with your heart, with your mind, with your brain, with your feelings, you cannot understand what truth is.

Questioner: Whatever I hear you say in this Hall becomes so simple and easy to understand. But the moment I am outside I am at sea—and I do not know what to do when I am alone.

KRISHNAMURTI: Sir, look: what the speaker has said is very clear. He is pointing out to you 'what is'—it is yours, it is not in this Hall, it does not lie with the speaker; the speaker is not making any propaganda, he does not want a thing from you, neither your flattery, nor your insults nor your applause. It is yours, your life, your misery, your despair; that you have to understand, not just here, because here you are being pushed into a corner, you are facing yourself perhaps for a few minutes. But when you leave the Hall, that is where the fun begins! We are not trying to influence you to act, to think, to do this or that—that would be propaganda. But if you have listened with your heart and with a mind that is aware—not influenced—if you have observed, then when you go outside it will go with you wherever you are because it is yours, you have understood.

Questioner : *What is the role of the artist?*

KRISHNAMURTI : Are artists so very different from other human beings? Why do we divide life into the scientist, the artist, the housewife, the doctor? The artist may be a little more sensitive, may observe more, he may be more alive. But he also has his problems as a human being. He may produce marvellous pictures, or write lovely poems, or make things with his hands, but he is still a human being, anxious, frightened, jealous and ambitious. How can an 'artist' be ambitious? If he is, he is no longer an artist. The violinist or the pianist who uses his instrument to make money, to gain prestige—just think of it—is not a musician. Or the scientist who works for governments, for society, for war, is he a scientist? That man who is seeking knowledge and understanding has become corrupt like other human beings. He may be marvellous in his laboratory or he may express himself on a canvas most beautifully, but he is torn inside like the rest, he is petty, shoddy, anxious, frightened. Surely an artist, a human being, an individual, is a whole, indivisible, complete thing. Individual means undivided; but we are not, we are broken-up, fragmented, human beings—the businessman, the artist, the doctor, the musician. And therefore we lead a life— Oh I do not have to describe it, you know it.

Questioner : *Sir, what is the criterion in choosing between various possibilities.*

KRISHNAMURTI : Why do you choose at all? When you see

something very clearly, what is the need for choice? Do please listen to this. It is only a mind that is confused, uncertain, unclear, that chooses. I am not talking of choosing between red and black, but choosing psychologically. Unless you are confused, why should you choose? If you see something very clearly without any distortion, is there any need for choosing? There are no alternatives; alternatives exist when you have to choose between two physical roads—you may go one way or the other. But alternatives exist also in a mind that is divided in itself and is confused; therefore it is in conflict, therefore it is violent. It is the violent mind that says it will live peacefully and in its reaction it becomes violent. But when you see the whole nature of violence very clearly, from the most brutal to the most subtle form of violence, then you are free of it.

Questioner: When can you ever see it all?

KRISHNAMURTI: Have you observed a tree totally?

Questioner: I do not know.

KRISHNAMURTI: Sir, do it some time if you are interested in this kind of thing.

Questioner: I always thought I had, until the next time.

KRISHNAMURTI: To go into it, let us begin with the tree, which is the most objective thing. Observe it completely, which means without the observer, without the division —which does not mean you identify yourself with the tree, you do not become the tree, that would be too absurd. But to observe it implies to look at it without the division between you and the tree, without the space created by the 'observer' with his knowledge, with his thoughts, with his prejudice about that tree; not when you are angry, jealous, or in despair, or full of a thing called hope—which is the opposite of despair, therefore it is not hope at all. When you observe it, see it without the division, without that space, then you can see the whole of it.

When you observe your wife, your friend, your husband or whatever you will, when you look without the image, which is the accumulation of the past, you will see what an extraordinary thing takes place. You have never seen anything like that before in your life. But to observe totally implies no division. People take L.S.D. and other drugs in order to destroy the space between the observer and the observed. I have not taken it; and once you start that game you are lost, you are everlastingly dependent on it and it brings its own mischief.

Questioner: What is the relationship between thought and reality?

KRISHNAMURTI: What is thought in relationship to time, thought in relationship to what is measurable and what is immeasurable? What is thought? Thought is the response of memory—obviously. If you had no memory you would not be able to think at all, you would be in a state of amnesia. Thought is always old, thought is never free, thought can never be new. When thought is silent there may be a new discovery; but thought cannot possibly discover anything new. Is this clear? Please do not agree with me. When you ask a question and you are familiar with that question, your response is immediate. 'What is your name'?—you reply immediately. 'Where do you live'?—you reply instantly. But a more complex question takes time. In that interval thought is looking, trying to remember.

So thought in its desire to find what truth is, is always looking in terms of the past. That is the difficulty of search. When you seek, you must be able to recognise what you have found; and what you find in terms of your recognition is the past. So thought is time—obviously—this is so simple, is it not? You had an experience yesterday of great delight, you think about it and you want it repeated again tomorrow. Thought thinking about something that has brought pleasure, wants it tomorrow; therefore 'tomorrow' and 'yesterday' make the time-interval in which you are going to get that pleasure, in which you are going to think about it. So thought is time. And thought can never be free because it is the response of the past. How can thought find out anything new? This is possible only when the mind is completely silent. Not because it wants to find something new, for then that silence is brought about by a motive and therefore it is not silence.

If you understand this you have understood the whole thing and even answered your question. You see, we are always using thought as a means of finding, of asking, of enquiring, looking. Do you mean to say thought can know what love is? Thought can know the pleasure of what it has called love and demand that pleasure again in the name of love. But thought, being the product of time, the product of measure, cannot possibly understand or come upon that thing which is not measurable. So then the question arises : how can you *make* thought silent? You cannot. Perhaps we will go into that another time.

Questioner : Do we need rules to live by?

KRISHNAMURTI : Madame, you have not heard all that I have been saying during this talk! Who is going to lay down the rules? The Churches have done it, tyrannical governments have done it, or you yourself have laid down the rules for your own conduct, for your own behaviour. And you know what that means—a battle between what you think you should be and what you are. Which is more important: to understand what you should be, or what you are?

Questioner: What am I?

KRISHNAMURTI: Let us find out. I have told you what you are—your country, your furniture, your images, your ambitions, your respectability, your race, your idiosyncrasies and prejudices, your obsessions—you know what you are! Through all that you want to find truth, God, reality. And because the mind does not know how to be free of all this you invent something, an outside agency, or give significance to life.

So when you understand the nature of thought—not verbally, but are actually aware of it—then when you have a prejudice, look at it and you will see that your religions are a prejudice, the identification with your country is a prejudice. We have so many opinions, so many prejudices; just observe one completely, with your heart, with your mind, with love —care for it, look at it. Do not say 'I must not' or 'I must'— just look at it. And then you will see how to live without any prejudice. It is only a mind that is free from prejudice, from conflict, that can see what truth is.

London. 27 May 1970.

10

THE RELIGIOUS MIND

'The religious mind is a light to itself. Its light is not lit by another—the candle that is lit by another can be put out very quickly.'

SHALL WE TALK about meditation? Talking about something and doing it are quite different things. If we are going to go into this complex problem, we not only have to understand the meaning of words, but also, it seems to me, we must go beyond the words. There are several things involved in meditation. To really understand it, to actually do it, not merely intellectually or verbally or theoretically, requires a peculiar kind of seriousness in which there must be a great deal of intelligence and humour.

First of all, one must enquire into what the religious mind is; not what religion is, but that quality of the mind and the heart that is religious. One can give a great many meanings to that word 'religion', depending on one's conditioning—either accepting it emotionally, sentimentally or devotionally, or totally denying the whole question of a religious attitude, a religious way of life, as a great many people do. One is rather ashamed even to talk about religious matters. But the religious mind has nothing whatsoever to do with belief in God—it has no theory, philosophy, or conclusion, because it has no fear and therefore no need for belief.

A religious mind is difficult to describe—the description can never be the thing described. But if one is sensitive, aware and serious, one can feel one's way into it.

First of all, one cannot belong to any organised religion.

123

I think that is one of the most difficult things for most human beings; they want to cling to some kind of hope, belief, some kind of theory or conclusion, or an experience of their own, giving it a religious significance. Any kind of attachment and therefore dependence on one's particular, secret experience or the accumulated experience of the so-called saints, the mystics, or your own particular guru or teacher, all that must be completely and wholly set aside. I hope you are doing it, because a religious mind is not burdened with fear, or seeking out any form of security and pleasure. A mind that is not burdened with experience is absolutely necessary to find out what meditation is. In seeking experience lies the way to illusion.

Not to seek any form of experience is very difficult; most of our lives are so mechanical, so shallow, that we want deeper experiences because we are bored with the superficiality of life. We want, or rather crave for, something that will have a meaning, a fullness, depth, beauty, loveliness, and so the mind is seeking. And what it seeks it will find; what it finds will not be the truth. Are you accepting all this, or rejecting it? Please do not accept or deny—this is not a matter of your pleasure or my pleasure, because in this there is no authority whatsoever, neither that of the speaker nor of anybody else. You see, most of us want someone to lead us, to guide us, to help us and we invest faith, trust, in that person or in that ideal or principle or image. Therefore we depend on another. A mind that is dependent on authority and therefore incapable of standing alone, incapable of understanding, incapable of looking directly, such a mind must inevitably have fear of going wrong, of not doing the right thing, of not reaching the ecstasy that is promised or that one hopes for. All such forms of authority must absolutely come to an end; which means to have no fear, no dependency on another (there is no guru) and a mind that is not seeking experience. Because when one wants an experience, it indicates that one wants—great pleasure, call it what you like—ecstasy, enjoyment, seeking truth, finding enlightenment.

Also, how does the seeker know what he has found and if what he has found is the truth? Can the mind that is seeking, searching, find something that is alive, moving, that has no resting place? The religious mind does not belong to any group, any sect, any belief, any church, any organised circus; therefore it is capable of looking at things directly and understanding things immediately. Such is the religious mind, because it is a light to itself. Its light is not lit by another—the candle that is lit by another can be put out very quickly. And most of our beliefs, dogmas, rituals, are the result of propaganda which has nothing whatsoever to do with a religious life. A religious mind is a light to itself and therefore there is no punishment or reward.

Meditation is the emptying of the mind, totally. The content of the mind is the result of time, of what is called evolution; it is the result of a thousand experiences, a vast accumulation of knowledge, of memories. The mind is so burdened with the past because all knowledge is the past, all experience *is* the past, and all memory is the accumulated result of a thousand experiences—that is the known. Can the mind, which is both the conscious as well as the unconscious, empty itself completely of the past? That is the whole movement of meditation. The mind being aware of itself without any choice, seeing all the movement of itself—can that awareness totally empty the mind of the known? Because if there is any remnant of the past the mind cannot be innocent. So meditation is the total emptying of the mind.

So many things are said about meditation, especially in the East; there are so many schools, so many disciplines, so many books written on how to meditate, what to do. How do you know if what is being said is true or false? When the speaker says meditation is the complete emptying of the mind, how do you know it is true? What tells you? Your personal prejudice, your particular idiosyncrasy of liking the face of the man who speaks?—or his reputation, or because he has got some empathy, a certain friendliness? How do you know? Must you go through all the systems, all the schools, have teachers who teach you how to meditate, before you find out what meditation is? Or can you find that out if you have none of these people to tell you what to do?

I am saying this most undogmatically: do not listen to anybody—including the speaker, especially the speaker—because you are very easily influenced, because you are all wanting something, craving for something, craving for enlightenment, for joy, for ecstasy, for heaven; you are caught very easily. So you have to find it out completely by yourself. Therefore there is no need to go to India, or to any Zen Buddhist monastery, to meditate, or to look to any teacher; because if you know how to look, everything is in you. Therefore you put aside completely all authority, all looking to anybody, because truth does not belong to anybody, it is not a personal matter. Meditation is not a private, personal pleasure or experience.

One can see that one needs great harmony between the mind, the heart and the body, if you can so divide it—psychosomatically, if you prefer it. Obviously there must be complete harmony, because if there is any contradiction, any division, then there is conflict. Conflict is the very essence of waste of energy and you need tremendous energy to meditate. Therefore harmony is necessary so that the mind, the brain, the organism and the depth of the heart are whole, not broken up; you can see that for yourself, nobody need teach you that. How to bring about that harmony is quite a different matter. Complete harmony means that the mind as well as the organism must be extraordinarily sensitive; therefore one has to go into the whole question of diet, exercise, and living properly. Because we do not want to think about it or look into it, we turn to somebody else to tell us what to do. And if we look to somebody else we limit our energy, because then we ask whether it is possible or not possible. If we say it is impossible, our energy becomes very limited; if we say it is possible in terms of what we already know, it becomes very small, and so on.

So one realises the necessity of this complete harmony, because if there is any kind of discord, there is distortion. And there must be discipline. Discipline means order—not suppression, not conformity to a principle or to an idea, to a conclusion, to a system or to a method.

Order is not a design, a pattern according to which you are living. Order comes only when you understand the whole process of disorder—going through what is the negative to come to the positive. Our life is disorder, which means contradiction, saying one thing, doing another and thinking something entirely different. It is a fragmentary existence, and in this fragmentation we try to find some kind of order. We think this order comes about through discipline and control. A mind that is controlled, disciplined in the sense of conforming to a pattern, whether established by oneself, or by society, or by a particular culture, such a mind is not free, it is a distorted mind. Therefore one has to enquire into this question of disorder. And through the understanding of what disorder is, how it comes about, there comes order—a living thing.

What is the very essence of disorder? Our lives are disorderly, divided; we live in different compartments; we are not a whole, unbroken entity. The essence of disorder is contradiction, and where there is contradiction in ourselves there must be effort and therefore disorder. (This is very simple. Probably you do not like simple things. One can make it very complex!) One sees how disorderly one's own life is, how the contradictions of various desires, purposes, conclusions, intentions, are tearing at each other; being violent, wanting to live peacefully; being ambitious, greedy, competitive and saying that one loves; being self-centered, egotistic, limited and talking about universal brotherhood. We pretend, and thus there is great hypocrisy.

So order is necessary and the very understanding of disorder brings about its own discipline, which is order in which there is no suppression, no conformity. I hope the speaker is making it clear, at least verbally. Discipline means to learn, not to accumulate mechanical knowledge—to learn about the disorderly life one leads and therefore not to come to any conclusion at any moment. Most of our actions are based on conclusions or on ideals or approximation to an ideal. So our actions are always contradictory and therefore disorderly. This one can see very easily. If one is looking at this in oneself, there will naturally come about order, freedom from all authority and therefore freedom from fear. One can make a mistake but correct it immediately.

How can the mind not be caught in illusion?—because you can 'meditate' endlessly, creating your own illusions. We met a man the other day who had meditated for twenty-five years—not casually—he had given up everything, his good position, money, family, name, and for twenty-five years he practised meditation. Unfortunately somebody brought him to one of the Talks and the next day he came to see the speaker and said : 'What you said about meditation is perfectly true : I have been hypnotising myself, having my own visions, having my own personal delight in these visions according to my conditioning.' If one is a Christian, one has visions of Christ and so on; if one is a Hindu one has one's own particular God and is directly in communication with him, which means, according to one's conditioning.

So the question is, how can the mind be totally free of illusion? One has to ask this question very seriously and deeply. A great many people listen to all kinds of yogis and teachers who tell them what to do, giving them some slogan, some mantra, some word that will give them extraordinary experiences—you know what the speaker is talking about. Have you ever listened so completely to a tone of music, that every other sound dies away except that one sound? If the mind pursues that sound, goes with it, you get extraordinary results. But that is not meditation, that is a kind of trick that one can play upon oneself and it is another form of illusion. Also taking drugs in order to have a 'transcendental experience' can, through chemistry, bring about certain results; just as, if you fast a great deal, you have a certain sensitivity and your mind becomes much more alert, watchful, sharp and clear—or if you go in for breathing properly. These are various forms of tricks, bringing about their own illusion. And the mind clings to those illusions, because they are very satisfactory, they are your private, personal achievement. But when the world is suffering, going through agony, distortion, corruption, your particular little vision in a small corner of the field has no value.

So, one can brush aside all that as being immature and childish. Besides, it leads to stupor, it makes the mind dull. Now, how is the mind to be free of all illusion?—bearing in mind that if there is any effort and any contradiction there must be illusion. How can that state of contradiction, that confusion, distortion, the various forms of corruption—social, religious and personal corruptions—how can all that which induces various forms of delusions and illusions be completely wiped away? This can only happen when the mind is completely still, because any movement of thought is a movement of the past. Thought is the reaction of memory, of accumulated experience, knowledge and so on—it is the past. And as long as that movement of the past exists in the whole structure of the mind—which includes the brain—there must be distortion.

So the question is : how can thought be totally absent in meditation? Thought is necessary; the more it is logical, sane, healthy, objective, unemotional, impersonal, the more effective and efficient it is. You must use thought to function in life. And yet the mind must be capable, must be completely free of any sense of distortion to find out what is true, what is sacred. There must be harmony between the living functioning in thought and the freedom from thought. This is logical;

this is not some cryptic, personal theory. To see anything that is true, that is new to be discovered, new to be perceived, something that has not been created or done before, the mind must be free from the known. And yet one has to live in the known. The man who came upon the jet engine, must have been free of the knowledge of the internal combustion engine. So in the same way, for the mind to come upon something that is totally new, there must be no illusion, there must be complete, total silence; not only in the movement of thought, but also in the very activity of the brain-cells themselves with their memories.

That is quite a problem, is it not? Do you understand the way we live in formulas, in conclusions, in prejudices? We live mechanically, in the routine of earning a livelihood, the routine of function from which we try to derive a position and prestige. Our life is a series of conformities; there is either the conformity of fear or the conformity of pleasure. Such a mind cannot possibly come upon anything new. Therefore any teacher, any method, any system that says, 'Do this and you will find it', is telling you a lie. Because anyone who says he knows, he does not know. What he knows is the routine, the practice, the discipline, the conformity.

So the mind and the brain and the body in complete harmony must be silent—a silence that is not induced by taking a tranquilliser or by repeating words, whether it be Ave Maria or some Sanskrit word. By repetition your mind can become dull, and a mind which is in a stupor cannot possibly find what is true. Truth is something that is new all the time—the word 'new' is not right, it is really 'timeless'.

So there has to be silence. That silence is not the opposite of noise or the cessation of chattering; it is not the result of control, saying 'I will be silent', which again is a contradiction. When you say 'I will', there must be an entity who determines to be silent and therefore practises something which he calls silence; therefore there is a division, a contradiction, a distortion.

All this requires great energy and therefore action. We waste a great deal of energy in accumulating knowledge. Knowledge has its own place—you must have knowledge, the more of it the better. But when it becomes mechanical, when knowledge makes the mind feel that no more is possible, when we come to the conclusion that it is not possible to change, then we have no energy.

There is the idea of sexual control in order to have more energy to find God, and all the religious implications of it. Think of all those poor saints and monks, what tortures they go through to find God! And God—if there is such a thing— does not want a tortured mind, a mind that is torn apart, distorted or that has become dull and lives in stupefaction.

Silence of the mind comes naturally—please do listen to this—it comes naturally, easily, without any effort if you know how to observe, how to look. When you observe a cloud, look at it without the word and therefore without thought, look at it without the division as the observer. Then there is an awareness and attention in the very act of looking; not the determination to be attentive, but looking with attention, even though that look may last only a second, a minute —that is enough. Do not be greedy, do not say, 'I must have it for the whole day'. To look without the observer means looking without the space between the observer and the thing observed—which does not mean identifying oneself with the thing that is looked at.

So when one can look at a tree, at a cloud, at the light on the water, without the observer, and also—which is much more difficult, which needs a greater attention—if you can look at yourself without the image, without any conclusion, because the image, the conclusion, the opinion, the judgment, the goodness and the badness, is centred round the observer, then you will find that the mind, the brain, becomes extra-ordinarily quiet. And this quietness is not a thing to be cultivated; it can happen, it *does* happen, if you are attentive, if you are capable of watching all the time, watching your gestures, your words, your feelings, the movements of your face and all the rest of it. To correct it brings contradiction, but if you watch it, this brings about alteration by itself.

So silence comes about when there is profound attention, not only at the conscious level but also at the deeper levels of consciousness. Dreams and sleep are of great importance; it is part of meditation to be awake in sleep, to be aware, attentive while the mind and the body—the organism—is asleep. (Please, do not accept anything the speaker says—the speaker is not your guru, your teacher or your authority. If you make of him your authority, you are destroying yourself and the speaker.)

We said : meditation is the emptying of the mind; not only the conscious mind but also all the hidden layers of the mind, which are called the unconscious. The unconscious is as trivial and absurd as the conscious. And during sleep there are various kinds of superficial dreams, not even worth thinking about—dreams that have no meaning at all. I am sure you know all about this, do you not? Then there is the dream which has meaning, and that meaning can be understood as it is being dreamt. This is only possible when during the day you are attentive, watching, listening to every movement of your thoughts, motives, feelings and ambitions. Watching does not tire you, does not exhaust you, if you do not correct what you watch. If you say, 'This must not be' or, 'It must be', then you get tired and bored. But if you watch choicelessly, are aware without like or dislike during the day, then when you dream and those dreams have some significance, at the very moment of dreaming—all dreams are active, there is always some action taking place—that very action is understood. So when you have done all this, the mind in sleep becomes extraordinarily awake and you do not have to go to an analyser of dreams. That wakefulness of the mind sees something which the conscious mind can never see. So silence is not a thing to be practised—it comes when you have understood the whole structure and the beginning and the living of life.

We have to alter the structure of our society, its injustice, its appalling morality, the divisions it has created between man and man, the wars, the utter lack of affection and love that is destroying the world. If your meditation is only a personal matter, a thing which you personally enjoy, then it is not meditation. Meditation implies a complete radical change of the mind and the heart. This is only possible when there is this extraordinary sense of inward silence, and that alone brings about the religious mind. That mind knows what is sacred.

Questioner: How can we make this complete change?

KRISHNAMURTI : Sir, can knowledge bring about a total revolution?—can the past, which is knowledge, bring about a complete change in the quality of the mind? Or must there be freedom from the past, so that the mind is in constant revolution, in constant movement of change? The centre of knowledge, of experience, of memory, is in the observer, is it not? Please do not accept this, just watch it for yourself. There is the censor, the ego in each one, who says, 'This is right', 'This is wrong', 'This is good', 'This is bad', 'I must', 'I should not'. That censor is observing. He is the observer and he divides himself from the thing he observes. The censor, the observer, is always the past and the 'what is' is always changing, new. As long as there is this division between the observer and the observed, no radical revolution is possible : there will always be corruption. You can see what the French Revolution or what the Communist Revolution has done—corruption comes in all the time. As long as this division exists, goodness is not possible. Then you will say, 'How is this division to come to an end?' How can the observer, who is the accumulated past as knowledge, come to an end? It cannot come to an end because you need the 'observer' when you are functioning mechanically. You need knowledge when you go to the office or to the factory, or to the laboratory. But that knowledge, tied to the censor who is ambitious and greedy, becomes corrupt; he uses knowledge for corruption. This is so simple!

When there is a realisation of this, then the 'observer' comes to an end; it is not a matter of time, of the observer gradually coming to an end. We are conditioned to think, 'Gradually we will get rid of the observer, gradually we will become non-violent.' But in the meantime we sow the seeds of violence.

So when you see very clearly how the 'observer' distorts everything—the observer being the ego, the 'me'—how it separates and distorts, in that flash of perception the observer is not.

Questioner: Is it possible for continuous harmony to exist in this life?

KRISHNAMURTI: Continuous harmony in this life is a contradiction, is it not? The idea that it must be continuous prevents the discovery of anything new. Only in ending is there a new beginning. So the desire to have continuous harmony is a contradiction. You are harmonious—full stop. We are slaves to the word 'to be'. If anything which you call harmony has continuity, it is disharmony. Therefore, sir, do not wish for anything continuous. You want your relationship with your wife to be continuous, happy, lovely—all the romantic things. And it never happens. Love is not something that is of time. So do not let us be greedy. Harmony is not a thing that can continue. If it continues it becomes mechanical. But a mind that is harmonious '*is*'—not 'will be' or 'has been'. A mind that is harmonious—again, '*is*' is the wrong word—a mind that is aware that it is harmonious does not ask the question, 'Will I have it tomorrow?'

Questioner: Sir, how are things related to the verbal content of the mind?

KRISHNAMURTI : It is very simple, is it not? When we understand that the word is not the thing, that the description is not the described, the explanation is not the explained, then the mind is free of the word. If one has an image about oneself, the image is put together by words, by thought—thought is the word. One thinks of oneself as big, or small, clever, or a genius or whatever you will—one has an image about oneself. That image can be described, it is the result of description. And that image is the creation of thought. But is the description, the image, part of the mind? What relationship has the content of the mind to the mind itself? Is the content the mind itself?—is that the question, sir? Of course it is. If the content of the mind is furniture, books, what people say, your prejudices, your conditioning, your fears, that is the mind. If the mind says there is a soul, there is God, there is hell, there is heaven, there is a devil, that is the content of the mind. The content of the mind *is* the mind. If the mind can empty itself of all that, it is something entirely different; then the mind is something new and therefore immortal.

Questioner: What is the sign of a man who has begun to develop awareness?

KRISHNAMURTI : I'm sorry, I want to be funny about it—he doesn't carry a red flag! Look, sir, first of all, as we said, it is not a matter of development, it is not a matter of slow growth. Does it need time to understand something? What is the state of the mind that says, 'I've understood'—not verbally but totally? When does it say this? It says it when the mind is really completely attentive to the thing it is looking at. Being attentive at that moment it has understood completely, it is not a matter of time.

Questioner: There is so much suffering; having compassion, how can one be at peace?

KRISHNAMURTI: Do you think you are different from the world? Are you not the world?—the world that you have made with your ambition, with your greed, with your economic securities, with your wars—you made it. The torture of animals for your food, the wastage of money on war, the lack of right education—you have built this world, it is part of you. So you are the world and the world is you; there is no division between you and the world. You ask, 'How can you have peace when the world suffers?' How can you have peace when you are suffering? This is the question, because you are the world. You can go all over the world, talk to human beings, whether they are clever, famous or illiterate, they are all going through a terrible time—like you. So the question is not, 'How can you have peace when the world is suffering?' You are suffering and therefore the world suffers; therefore put an end to your suffering, if you know how to end it. Suffering with its self-pity comes to an end only when there is self-knowing. And you will say, 'What can one human being do who has freed himself from his own sorrow, what value has that human being in the world?' Such a question has no value. If you have freed yourself from sorrow—do you know what that means?—and say, 'What value has the individual in a suffering world?', that is a wrong question.

Questioner: What is madness?

KRISHNAMURTI: Oh, that is very clear. Most of us are neurotic, are we not? Most of us are slightly off balance, most of us have peculiar ideas, peculiar beliefs. Once we were talking to a very devout Catholic and he said, 'You Hindus are the most superstitious, bigoted and neurotic people; you believe in so many abnormal things.' He was totally unaware of his own abnormality, his own beliefs, his own stupidities. So who is balanced? Obviously, the man who has no fear, who is whole. Whole means sane, healthy and holy; but we are not, we are broken-up human beings, therefore we are unbalanced. There is only balance when we are completely whole. That means healthy, with a mind that is clear, that has no prejudice and that has goodness. (*Applause.*) Please do not clap, your applause has no meaning to me—I mean it. If you have understood it, because you have seen it for yourself, then there is no need to applaud—it is yours. Enlightenment does not come through another, it comes through your own observation, your own understanding of yourself.

London. 30 May 1970.

PART IV

11

THE UNCONDITIONED MIND

'A mind that is caught up in knowledge as a means to freedom does not come to that freedom.'

I F Y O U A R E at all serious, the question whether it is possible to uncondition the mind, must be one of the most fundamental. One observes that man, in different parts of the world, with different cultures and social moralities, is very deeply conditioned; he thinks along certain lines, he acts and works according to pattern. He is related to the present through the background of the past. He has cultivated great knowledge; he has millions of years of experience. All this has conditioned him—education, culture, social morality, propaganda, religion—and to this he has his own particular reaction; the response of another form of conditioning.

One has to be sufficiently attentive to see the whole significance of this conditioning, how it divides people, nationally, religiously, socially, linguistically. These divisions are a tremendous barrier, they breed conflict and violence. If one is to live completely at peace, creatively—we will go into the words 'peace' and 'creatively' presently—if one is to live that way, one must understand this conditioning which is not only peripheral or superficial, but also very deep, hidden. One has to discover whether the whole structure of this conditioning can be revealed. And when that is discovered, what is one to do, to go beyond it?

If one observes that one is conditioned and says, 'One can never possibly uncondition the mind', the problem ends. If you start out with a formula that one will never be unconditioned, all enquiry ceases, one has already resisted and answered the problem and there it ends; then one can only further decorate the conditioning. But if one goes into this fairly deeply and one becomes aware of the whole problem, then what is one to do? How does one respond if this is a very, very serious challenge and not something that one just brushes aside? If it is something vital and tremendously important in one's life, what is one's response?

If you have discovered this conditioning then what is the manner of your observation? Have you observed it for yourself or has somebody told you about it? This is really quite an important question to answer. If you have been told about it and you say, 'Yes, I am conditioned', then you are responding to a suggestion; it is not real, it is only a verbal concept which you have accepted, with which you agree; that is quite different from the discovery of it for yourself, for then it is tremendously vital and you have the passion to find the way out of it.

Have you discovered that you are conditioned because you have enquired, searched and looked into it? If so: 'who' has discovered it?—the observer, the examiner, the analyser?— 'who' is observing, examining, analysing the whole mess and the madness that this conditioning is causing in the world? 'Who' by observing has discovered the structure of this conditioning and its result? By observing what is happening, outwardly and inwardly—the conflicts, the wars, the misery, the confusion in oneself and outside oneself (the outside is part of what one is)—by observing this very closely (all over the world this thing is happening) I have discovered that I am conditioned and have found the consequence of this conditioning. So: there is the 'observer' who has discovered that he is conditioned, and the question arises: is the 'observer' different from that which he has observed and discovered, is that something separate from himself? If there is separation, then again there is division and therefore conflict as to how to overcome this conditioning, how to free oneself from this conditioning, what to do about it and so on. One has to discover whether there are two separate things, two separate movements, the 'observer' and that which is observed. Are they separate? Or is the 'observer' the observed? It is tremendously important to find this out for oneself; if one does, then the whole way one thinks undergoes a complete change. It is a most radical discovery as a result of which the structure of morality, the continuation of knowledge, has, for oneself, quite a different meaning. Find out if you have discovered this for yourself, or whether you have accepted what you have been told as fact, or whether you have discovered this for yourself without any outside agency telling you 'It is so'. If it is your discovery, it releases tremendous energy, which before had been wasted in the division between the 'observer' and the observed.

The continuation of knowledge (psychological conditioning) in action is the wastage of energy. Knowledge has been gathered by the 'observer' and the 'observer' uses that knowledge in action, but that knowledge is divided from action; hence here is conflict. And the entity that holds this knowledge—which is essentially his conditioning—is the 'observer'. One must discover this basic principle for oneself; it is a *principle*, not something fixed; it is a reality which can never be questioned again.

What happens to a mind that has discovered this truth, this simple fact, that the 'observer' is the observed—psychologically speaking? If this is discovered, what takes place to the quality of the mind—which has for so long been conditioned by its concepts of the 'Higher Self' or the 'Soul' as something divided from the body? If this discovery does not open the door to freedom it has no meaning; it is still just another intellectual notion, leading nowhere. But if it is an actual discovery, an actual reality, then there must be freedom —which is not the freedom to do what you like or the freedom to fulfil, to become, to decide, or the freedom to think what you like and act as you wish.

Does a free mind choose? Choice implies decision between this and that; but what is the need of any choice at all? (Please, sirs, these are not verbal statements; we have to go into it, we have to live it daily and then will be found the beauty of it, the vigour, the passion, intensity of it.) Choice implies decision; decision is the action of will; who is the entity that exercises will to do this or that? Please follow this carefully. If the 'observer' is the observed, what need is there for decision at all? When there is any form of decision (psychologically), depending on choice, it indicates a mind that is confused. A mind that sees very clearly does not choose, there is only action—the lack of clarity comes into being when there is division between the 'observer' and the observed.

Questioner : Factually there has to be this choice, this division —does there not?

KRISHNAMURTI : I choose between brown cloth and red cloth —of course. But I am talking psychologically.

If one understands the effects of choice, the effects of division and decision, then the choosing becomes a very small affair. For example : I am confused; in this world I have been brought up as a Catholic, or as a Hindu; I am not satisfied and I jump into another religious organisation that I have 'chosen'. But if I examine the whole conditioning of a particular religious culture, I see that it is propaganda, a series of acceptances of beliefs, all arising through fear, through the demand for security, psychologically; because inwardly one is insufficient, miserable, unhappy, uncertain, one puts one's hope in something that can offer security, certainty. So when the particular religion to which I belong fails, I jump into another, hoping to find that security there; but it is the same thing under another name, whether called 'X' or 'Y'. When the mind is very clear about this, it understands the whole situation and it has no need of choice; then the whole response of action according to 'will' comes completely to an end. 'Will' implies resistance and is a form of isolation; a mind that is isolated is not a free mind.

A mind that is caught up in the acquisition of knowledge as a means to freedom does not come to that freedom. Why has knowledge become such an extraordinarily important thing in life?—knowledge being the accumulated experience of that which other people have discovered—scientific, psychological and so on, together with the knowledge one has acquired for oneself through observation, through learning. What place has knowledge in freedom? Knowledge is always of the past; when you say 'I know', it is implied that you *have known*. Knowledge of every kind, scientific, personal, communal, whatever it is, is always of the past; and as one's mind is the result of the past, can it be free at all?

Questioner : What about self-knowledge?

KRISHNAMURTI : See, first, how the mind accumulates knowledge and why it does so; see where knowledge is necessary, and where it becomes an impediment to freedom. Obviously to do anything one must have knowledge—to drive a car, to speak a language, to do a technological job—you must have abundance of knowledge, the more efficient, the more objective, the more impersonal, the better—but we are speaking of that knowledge which conditions one, psychologically.

The 'observer' is the reservoir of knowledge. The 'observer' therefore, is of the past, he is the censor, the entity that judges from accumulated knowledge. He does this with regard to himself. Having acquired knowledge about himself from the psychologists, he thinks he has learnt about himself and with that knowledge he looks at himself. He does not look at himself with fresh eyes. He says, 'I know, I have seen myself, parts are extraordinarily nice, but the other parts are rather terrible.' He has already judged and he never discovers anything new about himself because he, the 'observer', is separated from that which is observed, which he calls himself. That is what we are doing all the time, in all relationships. Relationships with another or relationships with the machine are all based on the desire to find a place where we can be completely secure, certain. And we seek security in knowledge; the keeper of this knowledge is the 'observer', the thinker, the experiencer, the censor, always as being different from the thing observed.

Intelligence is not in the accumulation of knowledge. The accumulation of knowledge is static—one may add to it but the core of it is static. From this static accumulation one lives, one functions, one paints, one writes, one does all the mischief in the world and one calls that freedom. So can the mind be free of knowledge, of the known? This is really quite an extraordinary question, if one asks it not merely intellectually, but really very, very deeply; can the mind ever be free of the known? Otherwise there is no creation; there is nothing new under the sun then; it is always reformation of the re-formed.

One has to find out why this division between the 'observer' and the observed exists; and can the mind go beyond this division, so as to be freed from the known to function in a different dimension altogether?—which means that intelligence will use knowledge when necessary and yet be free of knowledge.

Intelligence implies freedom; freedom implies the cessation of all conflict; intelligence comes into being and conflict comes to an end when the 'observer' is the observed, for then there is no division. After all, when this exists there is love. That word, so terribly loaded, one hesitates to use; love is associated with pleasure, sex and fear, with jealousy, with dependency, with acquisitiveness. A mind that is not free does not know the meaning of love—it may know pleasure and hence know fear, which are certainly not love.

Love can only come into being when there is real freedom from the past as knowledge. Is that ever possible? Man has sought this in different ways; to be free of the transiency of knowledge. He has always sought something beyond knowledge, beyond the response of thought; so he has created an image called God. All the absurdities that arise around that! But to find out if there is something that is beyond the imagery of thought there must be freedom from all fear.

Questioner : Are you differentiating between the brain as intellect and the mind; the mind being something other, an awareness?

KRISHNAMURTI : No, we are using the word 'mind' as meaning the total process of thought, as memory, as knowledge, including the brain cells.

Questioner : Including the brain cells?

KRISHNAMURTI : Obviously. One cannot separate the brain cells from the rest of the mind, can one? The brain—what is the function of the brain? A computer?

Questioner : Yes, I think so.

KRISHNAMURTI : A most extraordinary computer, put together over thousands of years; it is the result of thousands of years of experience, to secure survival and safety. And one has so much knowledge of everything that is happening in the outer world, but very little knowledge about oneself.

Questioner : Could not creation depend on memory and therefore depend on the past? You said earlier that there is in fact nothing new under the sun.

KRISHNAMURTI : 'There is nothing new under the sun'—at least the Bible, Ecclesiastes, says so. Are we not confusing creation with expression—and whether a creative person needs expression? Do think it out: 'I need to fulfil myself in something that must be expressed', 'I have a feeling that I am an artist and I must paint, or write a poem.' Does creation need expression at all? And does the expression of an artist indicate a mind that is free in creation? You understand? One writes a poem or paints a picture—does that indicate a creative mind? What does creativeness mean? Not the mechanical repetition of the past!

Questioner : I think creativeness does need expression or we would not have a world.

KRISHNAMURTI : Creativeness does need expression? What does creativeness mean? What is the feeling of the mind that is creative?

Questioner : When the mind is inspired; when it can make something good and beautiful.

KRISHNAMURTI : Does a creative mind need inspiration?
    Must not the mind be free to be creative—free? Otherwise it is repetitive. In that repetitiveness there may be new expressions but it is still repetitive, mechanical; a mind that is mechanical, can it be creative? The mind of a human being in conflict, in tension, neurotic—though writing marvellous poems, marvellous plays—can it be creative?

Questioner : It must be 'in the now' and not . . .

KRISHNAMURTI : What does it mean, to be 'in the now'? It

cannot be mechanical. It cannot be burdened with all the weight of knowledge, of tradition. It means a mind that is really, profoundly free—free of fear. That is freedom, is it not?

Questioner: But surely it must still seek safety; that is the function of the brain.

KRISHNAMURTI: Of course, it is the function of the brain to seek security. But is it secure when it conditions itself as to nationality and religious belief, in saying this is mine, that is yours and so on?

Questioner: It seems to me that without opposition there is no growth. It is part of neurology.

KRISHNAMURTI: Is it?

Questioner: Without high there is no low, or without wide there is no narrow.

KRISHNAMURTI: Let us find out We have lived that way, between the good and the bad, between hate, jealousy and love, between tenderness and brutality, between violence and gentleness, for millions of years. And we say we have accepted that because it is something real; is it, to live like that? The quality of mind that wavers between hate and jealousy and pleasure and fear, can it know what love means? Can a mind that is always seeking expression, fulfilment, seeking to become famous, to be recognised—which we call becoming, being, which is part of the social structure, part of our conditioning

149

—can such a mind be creative? When a mind is caught in always becoming something, in the verb 'to be', 'I will be', 'I have been', there is the fear of death, the fear of the unknown, so it clings to the known. Can such a mind ever be creative? Can creation result from stress, opposition, strain?

Questioner: Creativeness is joy, imagination.

KRISHNAMURTI: Do you know what joy means? Is joy pleasure?

Questioner: No.

KRISHNAMURTI: You say 'no'; but that is what you are seeking, are you not? You may have a moment of great ecstasy, great joy, and you think about it. Thinking about it reduces it to pleasure. We all so easily come to conclusions, and a mind that has reached conclusions is not a free mind. Find out whether one can live without any conclusions; live daily a life without comparisons. You conclude because you compare. Live a life without comparison; do it and you will find out what an extraordinary thing takes place.

Questioner: If there is just the experience and the experience is fear, or anger, what happens?

KRISHNAMURTI: If one lives only in an experience without that experience being recorded and recognised in the future as an experience, what happens? I think one has first to find out what we mean by that word 'experience'. Does it not mean 'to go through'? And does it not imply recognition, otherwise one would not know that one had had an experience? If I did not recognise the experience, would it be experienced?

150

Questioner: *Can there not be just the experience?*

KRISHNAMURTI : Go a little further. Why do we need experience at all? We all want experience; we are bored with life, we have made life into a mechanical affair and we want wider, deeper experiences, transcendental experiences. So there is the escape from this boredom, through meditation, into the so-called divine. Experience implies recognition of what has happened; you can only recognise if there is a memory of that thing which has already happened. So the question is : why do we seek experience at all? To waken us up, because we are asleep? Is it a challenge to which we respond according to our background, which is the known?

So, is it possible to live a life in which the mind is so clear, awake, a light to itself, that it needs no experience? That means to live a life without conflict; that means a mind that is highly sensitive and intelligent, which does not need something to challenge it or to awaken it.

Brockwood Park. 12 September 1970.

12

FRAGMENTATION AND UNITY

'For the stillness of the mind, its complete quiet, an extraordinary discipline is required; . . . the mind then has a religious quality of unity; from that there can be action which is not contradictory.'

ONE OF THE most important problems to solve is that of bringing about a complete unity, something beyond the fragmentary self-centred concern with the 'me', at whatever level it be, social, economic or religious. The 'me' and the 'not me', the 'we' and 'they' are the factors of division.

Is it ever possible to go beyond the activity of self-centred concern? If something is 'possible' then one has a great deal of energy; but what wastes energy is the feeling that it is not possible, so that one just drifts—as most of us do—from one trap to another. How is this possible?—recognising that in a human being there is a great deal of the animal aggression and violence, a great deal of the stupid mischievous activity; recognising how he is caught in various beliefs, dogmas and separatist theories and how he revolts against one particular system or establishment and falls into another.

So, seeing the human situation as it is, what is one to do? This, I think, is the question that every human being who is sensitive, alive and aware of the things that are happening around him, must inevitably ask. It is not an intellectual or hypothetical question but something arising from the actuality of living. It is not something for the few rare moments but something that persists throughout the day and night, through the years and until one lives a life that is completely harmonious, without conflict in oneself and with the world.

Conflict, as one observes, arises from self-centred concern, which gives such tremendous importance to the appetites. How does one go beyond this petty, shoddy, little self? (It *is* that, though one may call it the soul, the Atman—such pleasant sounding words that one invents to cover a corruption). How is one to go beyond?

Not being capable of inward changes, psychologically, we turn to outside agency—change the environment, the social and economic structure, and man will inevitably also change! That has proved utterly false—though the communists insist on that theory. And religious authorities have said : believe, accept, put yourself in the hands of something outside and greater than yourself. That too has lost its vitality because it is not real, it is merely an intellectual invention, a verbal structure which has no depth whatsoever. The identification of oneself with the nation, that too has brought dreadful wars, misery and confusion—ever-increasing division. Seeing all this, what is one to do?—escape to some monastery, learn Zen meditation, accept some philosophical theory and commit oneself to that, meditate as a means of escape and self-hypnosis? One sees all this—actually, not verbally or intellectually— and sees that it leads nowhere; does one not inevitably throw it all aside, deny it all, completely, totally?

One sees the absurdity of all forms of self-identification with something larger, of expecting the environment to shape man; one sees the falseness of it all; one sees the superficiality of beliefs, noble or ignoble; then does one not set all that aside, actually, not theoretically? If one does—and it is quite a task—it implies a mind that is capable of looking at things completely, as they are, without any distortion, without any interpretation according to one's like or dislike; then what takes place to the quality of the mind? Is there not immediate action?—action that is intelligence; the seeing of the danger and acting; intelligence in which there is no division between seeing and acting. In the very perception is action. When one does not act, insanity begins, imbalance takes place; then we say, 'I cannot do that, it is too difficult, what shall I do?'

When there is a concept according to which action is determined, psychologically, there is division and there must be conflict. This conflict between the idea and action is the most confusing factor in life. Is it not possible to act without the ideation taking place?—which is, seeing and the action taking place together; for when there is great physical danger, a crisis, that is what we do, act instantly. Is it possible to live like that? That is: is it possible to see clearly the danger, say, of nationalism, or of religious beliefs, which separate man against man, so that the very seeing of it is the understanding that it is false?—it is not a question of believing that it is false. Belief has nothing whatever to do with perception; on the contrary, belief prevents perception; if you have a formula, a tradition, or a prejudice, you are a Hindu, a Jew, an Arab or a Communist and so on, then that very division breeds antagonism, hate, violence, and you are incapable of seeing the actuality. In any division between the concept and action there must be conflict; this conflict is neurotic, insane. Can the mind see directly so that in the very seeing is the doing? That demands attention, that requires an alertness, a quickness of the mind, a sensitivity.

One sees this—that one needs to have a clear, sharp, sensitive, intelligent awareness—and then one asks, 'How am I to get it, to capture it?'—in that question there is already division. Whereas, when you see the actual fact of what is going on, then the very seeing of it is the action—I hope this is clear.

Every form of conflict, inwardly or outwardly—and there is really no division as the outer or the inner—is distortion. I do not think that one realises this sufficiently clearly. One is so accustomed to conflict and struggle; one even feels that when there is no conflict one is not growing, not developing, not creating, that one is not functioning properly. One wants resistance, yet not seeing the implication of resistance, which is division. So, can the mind act without resistance, without conflict, seeing that any form of friction, any form of resistance, implies division bringing about a neurotic, conflicting state?

When there is perception and action without concept, the activity of the centre, of the 'self', the 'me', the 'I', the 'ego', the 'libido'—whatever word one uses to describe that which is inside—the 'observer', the censor, the controller, the thinker, the experiencer and so on, comes to an end. The centre of all psychological ideation is the 'me' (not practical and scientific knowledge and so on). When there is any challenge, then the response from the centre as the 'me' is the response of the past. Whereas, in the instant seeing and the instant acting the 'self' does not enter at all.

The centre is the Hindu, the Arab, the Jew, the Christian, the Communist and so on; when that centre responds, it is the response of his past conditioning, is the result of thousands of years of propaganda, religious and social; and when it responds there must be conflict.

When one sees something very clearly and acts there is no division. One does not learn this from books; it is something one can only learn through self-knowing, something learnt direct, not second-hand.

Can man, realising the transiency of all things, find something that is not of time? The brain is the result of time; it has been conditioned through thousands of years. Its thought is the response of memory, knowledge, experience; that thought can never discover anything new because it is from that conditioning; it is always the old; it is never free. Anything that thought projects is within the field of time; it may invent God, it may conceive a timeless state, it may invent a heaven, but all that is still its own product and therefore of time, of the past, and unreal.

So man, as one observes, realising the nature of time—the psychological time in which thought has become so extraordinarily important—has everlastingly sought something beyond. He sets out to find this; he becomes trapped in belief; through fear he invents a marvellous deity. He may set out to find it through a system of meditation, a repetitive affair, which may make the mind somewhat quiet and dull. He may repeat mantras endlessly. In such repetition the mind becomes mechanical, rather stupid; it may fly off into some mystical, supernatural, transcendental something or other that it projects for itself. That is not meditation at all.

Meditation implies a mind that is so astonishingly clear that every form of self-deception comes to an end. One can deceive oneself infinitely; and generally meditation, so-called, is a form of self-hypnosis—the seeing of visions according to your conditioning. It is so simple : if you are a Christian you will see your Christ; if you are a Hindu you will see your Krishna, or whichever of the innumerable gods you have. But meditation is none of these things : it is the absolute stillness of the mind, the absolute quietness of the brain. The foundation for meditation has to be laid in daily life; in how one behaves, in what one thinks. One cannot be violent and meditate; that has no meaning. If there is, psychologically, any kind of fear, then obviously meditation is an escape. For the stillness of the mind, its complete quiet, an extraordinary discipline is required; not the discipline of suppression, conformity, or the following of some authority, but that discipline or learning which takes place throughout the day, about every movement of thought; the mind then has a religious quality of unity; from that there can be action which is not contradictory.

And also, in all this : what part do dreams play? The mind is never still; the incessant activity that goes on during the day continues during sleep. The worries, the travails, the confusion, the anxiety, the fears and the pleasures go on when one sleeps; they become more acutely symbolised in dreams. Can the mind be completely still during sleep? This is possible, but only when the travail of the day is understood at each minute so that it is finished and not carried over. If one is insulted or praised, finish with it as it happens, so that the mind is constantly freed of problems. Then as you sleep, a different kind of quality comes into being, the mind is completely at rest, one is not carrying over the business of the day, one ends it with each day.

If one has gone through all this one sees that meditation is that quality of mind that is completely free from all knowledge—but such a mind uses knowledge; because it is free from 'the known' it can use 'the known'; when it uses 'the known' it is sane, objective, impersonal, not dogmatic.

And so it happens that in this silence of the mind there is a quality which is timeless. But, as we said, the explanation, the description, is not that which is explained or described. Most of us are satisfied with explanations or descriptions; one must be free of the word, for the word is not the thing. When one lives that way, life has quite a different beauty; there is great love which is neither pleasure nor desire; for pleasure and desire are related to thought, and love is not the product of thought.

Questioner : When I observe myself, I see a very rapid movement of thought and feeling and I am unable to watch one thought to its conclusion.

KRISHNAMURTI : There is always a chain of events going on. What are you to do? When you watch and try to understand one thought, go to its very end, another arises; this goes on all the time. There is your problem : as you are watching you are the multiplication of thoughts, and you cannot finish one thought to its end. What are you to do? Put the question differently; why does the mind endlessly chatter—why does this soliloquy go on? What happens if it does not go on? Is the chattering the result of wanting to be occupied with something? If you are not occupied, what takes place? If you are

157

a housewife you are occupied with housekeeping, or you are occupied as a businessman—occupation has become a mania. Why is the mind demanding this occupation, this chattering? What happens if it does not chatter, if it is not occupied?—is there fear behind it? Fear of what?

Questioner : *Of being nothing?*

KRISHNAMURTI : Fear of being empty, being lonely, fear of becoming aware of all the turmoil in itself; therefore it must be occupied with something, as the monk is occupied with his saviour, his prayers; the moment he stops he is just like anybody else, there is fear. So you want to be occupied, and this implies a fear of finding out what you are. Until you solve that problem of fear you will chatter.

Questioner : *As I watch myself the fear increases.*

KRISHNAMURTI : Naturally. So the question is : not so much how to stop the increase of fear, but rather, can fear end?

What is fear? You may not feel fear as you are sitting here, so perhaps you may not be able to take that and examine it and learn from it now. But you can immediately perceive that you depend, can you not? You depend on your friend, on your book, on your ideas, on your husband; psychological dependency is there, constantly. Why do you depend? Is it because it gives you comfort, a sense of security and of well-being, companionship? When that dependency fails you become jealous, angry and all that follows. Or, you try to cultivate freedom from dependency, to become independent. Why does the mind do all this? Is it because in itself it is empty, dull, stupid, shallow?—through dependency it feels that it is something more.

The mind chatters because it has to be occupied with

something or other; this occupation varies from the highest occupation of the 'religious' man to the lowest occupation of the soldier and so on. The mind is obviously occupied because otherwise it might discover something of which it is deeply afraid, something which it may not be able to solve.

What is fear?—does it not relate to something I have done in the past, or something that I imagine might happen in the future?—the past incident and the future accident; the past illness and the future recurrence of the pain of it. Now it is thought that creates this fear; thought breeds fear, just as thought sustains and nourishes pleasure. Then can thought end?—can it come to an end so that it no longer gives a continuity to fear or to pleasure? We want pleasure, we want it to continue; but fear, let us put it away. We never see that the two go together.

It is the machinery of thinking that is responsible, that gives the continuity to pleasure and fear. Can this machinery stop? When you see the extraordinary beauty of a sunset, see it; but do not qualify it with thought, saying, 'I must treasure it in the memory, or have it again'. To see it and so end it, is action. Most of us live in inaction, therefore there is endless chattering.

Questioner: But when the chattering does go on, do you just observe it?

KRISHNAMURTI: That is, become aware of this chattering— without choice. Which means: do not try to suppress it, do not say 'it is wrong, or right', or 'I must get beyond'. As you watch chattering, you discover why it goes on. When you learn about chattering, it is finished, there is no resistance to chattering. Through negation you have the positive action.

Brockwood Park. 13 September 1970.

PART V

13

PSYCHOLOGICAL REVOLUTION

'Seeing this vast fragmentation both inwardly and outwardly, the only issue is that a human being must radically, profoundly, bring about in himself a revolution.'

L I F E I S S E R I O U S; one has to give one's mind and one's heart to it, completely; one cannot play with it. There are so many problems; there is so much confusion in the world; there is the corruption of society and the various religious and political divisions and contradictions. There is great injustice, sorrow and poverty—not only the poverty outside but the poverty inside. Any serious man—fairly intelligent and not just sentimentally emotional—seeing all this, sees the necessity of change.

Change is either a complete psychological revolution in the nature of the whole human being, or it is a mere attempt at the reformation of the social structure. The real crisis in the life of man, you and I, is whether such a complete psychological revolution can be brought about—independent of nationality and of all religious division.

We have built this society; our parents, and their parents before them, have produced this corrupt structure and we are the product of that. We are society, we are the world, and if we do not change ourselves radically, really very, very deeply, then there is no possibility of changing the social order. Most of us do not realise this. Everyone, especially the younger generation, says : 'We must change society'. We talk a great deal but we do nothing about it. It is we ourselves that have to change, not society—do please realise this. We have to bring about in ourselves, at the highest and at the deepest levels, a change in our whole way of thinking, living, feeling; then only is the social change possible—mere social revolution, the changing of the structure of society outwardly by physical revolution, inevitably brings about, as has been seen, dictatorship or the totalitarian state, which deny all freedom.

To bring about such a change in ourselves is a lifetime's work—not just something for a few days then to be forgotten—it is a constant application, a constant awareness of what is going on, within and without.

We have to live in relationship; without it we cannot possibly exist. To be related means to live totally, wholly; for this there must be in ourselves a radical transformation. How shall we radically transform ourselves? If this seriously interests you then we shall have communication with each other; we shall think together, feel and understand together. So: how can man, you and I, totally change? That is the question and nothing else is relevant—it is a question not only for the young but also for the old.

In this world there is tremendous agony, immense sorrow, war, brutality and violence; there is starvation of which you know nothing. One realises that there is so much that *can* be done but for the vast fragmentation that there is, in the political world with its many parties and in the many religions; they all talk about peace but deny it, for there can only be peace, reality and love, when there is no division.

So again, seeing this vast fragmentation both inwardly and outwardly, the only issue is that a human being must radically, profoundly, bring about in himself a revolution. This is a very serious problem, it is an issue that affects one's whole life; in it is involved meditation, truth, beauty, love. These are not just words. One has to find a way of living where they come into reality.

One of the most important things in life is love. But what

is called love is associated with sex, which has become so tremendously important; everything seems to revolve around sex. Why do human beings—right through the world, whatever their cultures be, whatever religious sanctions say—find sex so extraordinarily important?—and with it is associated the word 'love'—why?

When you look at your own life, you see how it has become mechanical; our education is mechanical; we acquire knowledge, information, which gradually becomes mechanical. We are machines, second-hand people. We repeat what others have said. We read enormously. We are the result of thousands of years of propaganda. We have become psychologically and intellectually mechanical. In a machine there is no freedom. Sex offers freedom; there for a few seconds is freedom, you have completely forgotten yourself and your mechanical life. So sex has become enormously significant; its pleasure you call love. But is love pleasure? Or is love something entirely different, something in which there is no jealousy, no dependency, no possessiveness?

One has to give one's life to find out what love means, just as one has to give one's whole life to find out what meditation is and what truth is. Truth has nothing whatsoever to do with belief.

Belief comes into being when there is fear. One believes in God because in oneself one is so completely uncertain. One sees the transient things of life—there is no certainty, there is no security, there is no comfort, but immense sorrow—so thought projects something with the attribute of permanency, called God, in which the human mind takes comfort. But that is not truth.

Truth is something that is to be found when there is no fear. Again, one has to give a great deal of attention to understand what fear is—both physical and psychological fear. One has these problems in life which one has not understood, which one has not transcended; thereby one continues a corrupt society, whose morality is immoral and in which virtue, goodness, beauty, love, of which we talk so much, soon become corrupt.

Will the understanding of these problems take time? Is change immediate? Or is it to be brought about through the evolution of time? If time is taken—that is to say, at the end of your life you have reached enlightenment—then in that time you continue to sow seeds of corruption, war, hatred. So can this radical inward revolution happen instantly? It can happen instantly when you see the danger of all this. It is like seeing the danger of a precipice, of a wild animal, of a snake; then there is instant action. But we do not see the danger of all this fragmentation which takes place when the 'self', the 'me', becomes important—and the fragmentation of the ' me' and the 'not me'. The moment there is that fragmentation in yourself there must be conflict; and conflict is the very root of corruption. So, it behoves one to find out for oneself the beauty of meditation, for then the mind, being free and unconditioned, perceives what is true.

To ask questions is important; it is not only that one exposes oneself, but in asking questions one will find for oneself the answer. If one puts the right question the right answer is in the question. One must question everything in life, one's short hair or long hair, one's dress, the way one walks, the way one eats, what one thinks, how one feels—everything must be questioned : then the mind becomes extraordinarily sensitive, alive and intelligent. Such a mind can love; such a mind alone knows what a religious mind is.

Questioner: What is the meditation of which you speak?

KRISHNAMURTI : Do you know anything of what meditation means even?

Questioner: I know there are various forms of meditation, but I do not know which one you speak of.

KRISHNAMURTI : A system of meditation is not meditation. A system implies a method, which you practise in order to achieve something at the end. Something practised over and over again becomes mechanical—does it not? How can a mechanical mind—which has been trained and twisted, tortured to comply to the pattern of what it calls meditation— hoping to achieve a reward at the end—be free to observe, to learn?

There are various schools, in India and further East, where they teach methods of meditation—it is really most appalling. It means training the mind mechanically; it therefore ceases to be free and does not understand the problem.

So when we use the word 'meditation' we do not mean something that is practised. We have no method. Meditation means awareness; to be aware of what you are doing, what you are thinking, what you are feeling, aware without any choice, to observe, to learn. Meditation is to be aware of one's conditioning, how one is conditioned by the society in which one lives, in which one has been brought up, by the religious propaganda—aware without any choice, without distortion, without wishing it were different. Out of this awareness comes attention, the capacity to be completely attentive. Then there is freedom to see things as they actually are, without distortion. The mind becomes unconfused, clear, sensitive; such meditation brings about a quality of the mind that is completely silent—of which quality one can go on talking, but it will have no meaning unless it exists.

Questioner: Will not this way lead to more isolation, more confusion?

KRISHNAMURTI : First of all : are not most human beings

terribly confused? Are you not very confused?—see the fact, know whether you are confused or not. A mind that is confused, whatever it does, brings about confusion. A mind that is confused says 'I will practise meditation,' or 'I will find out what love is'—how can a confused mind find anything, except its own projection of confusion. If one has realised this fact, then what shall one do?

One is confused and one tries to bring about a state of mind which is not confused. One tries this, that, ten different things —drugs, drink, sex, worship, escapes—you follow—throw bombs, anything. The first thing is to stop action, to stop doing something. Also, one must stop all movement away from confusion so that there is no action springing to, or away from, confusion. So all action then stops, there is only confusion. There is no escape from it, neither is there trying to find a way out of it, nor trying to replace that confusion by clarity; there is no movement of thought away from this, causing further confusion; thought is not concerned with action for the moment. Then the question arises : are you aware of this confusion as being something outside of you as the 'observer', or are you part of this confusion? Is the 'observer' different from the thing observed—the confusion? If the 'observer' is differentiated from the thing observed then there is a contradiction—that very contradiction is the cause of confusion. So, how the mind looks at this confusion is important. Does it observe it as something apart, separated from itself, or is the 'observer' the observed? Please do understand this most important thing. Once you have understood this you will see what a tremendous difference it makes in life; all conflict is removed. The 'observer' no longer says : 'I must change it', 'I must bring about clarity', 'I must overcome it', 'I must try to understand it', 'I must escape from it'. All such activity is that of the 'observer' who has separated himself from the confusion and has generated conflict between himself and the confusion.

Questioner: I admit my confusion.

KRISHNAMURTI: Ah! The moment you say 'I admit my confusion', there is an entity who admits it. You do not see the importance of this. I observe; in observing do I find I am observing as an outsider, or as part of this confusion? If I am part of this confusion the mind becomes completely quiet, there is no movement, I am still, I do not move away from it. Therefore, when there is no division between the 'observer' and the observed there is complete cessation of confusion.

And the other question that was asked: 'If I am to learn from myself, what happens when the world around me controls me, conscripts me, takes me to war, tells me what to do politically, economically, religiously? There are the psychologists and the gurus from the East—they all tell me what to do. If I obey—which is what they all want me to do, promising Utopia at the end of it, or Nirvana, Enlightenment or truth—then I become mechanical. The root meaning of the word 'obey' is to hear. By hearing constantly what other people tell me, I gradually slip into obedience. If I learn from myself, I also learn about others. And if the government asks me to join the army, I will do what I think is right at the moment I am asked. A free mind does not obey. A free mind is free because in itself there is no confusion. Then you will say, 'What is the good of having one individual, one human being, with such a mind when all about it there is corruption, confusion?' *Do you think you would ask such a question if you had such a mind?*

What is the meaning of having a mind so completely clear and unconfused?

Questioner: Surely there will be no words any more?

KRISHNAMURTI: Those are all your speculations, are they not? How do you know?

Questioner: Words are the basis of ideas. There would be no ideas any more and the mind would be free; then we would not have relationships, we would not seek any more. We would have silence, complete silence and we would understand. Everybody can have a free mind.

KRISHNAMURTI: I understand what you are saying very clearly.

But, first of all: are we concerned with the world as something separate from ourselves? Is the world 'you' actually—not theoretically 'you'? Do you feel the quality of a mind that says, 'I am the world, the world is me, the me and the world are not two separate entities'? The 'self' is divided from the community, the 'self' is against the world, the 'self' is against your friend, against your wife, your husband. The 'self' is important, is it not? And that 'self' is asking the question, 'What will the world be if there is no self'? Find out if you can live without the 'self' and then you will see the truth of it. Also there is the previous question: what is the good of one human being in the world having a clear, unspotted mind, free—what is the point of it? Now who is asking the question? He who is confused or he whose mind is clear, unconfused, free? 'Who' is asking this question? Does the flower ask this question? Does love ask this question? Do you ask a question of this kind when you are confronted with a tremendous issue? Do you ask this question: what value is it if I know what it means to love when the others do not know what it means to love? You just love. You do not ask this question. When you have no fear, psychologically, and everyone around you has this fear, will you then ask: 'What is the good of my having no fear when all the others have fear?' Then what do you do? You have no fear and others have fear—what do you do?— you try to help me to learn the whole structure of fear.

Questioner: How do you prevent language creating division?

Each language has its own peculiar structure, a certain pattern, and language becomes a barrier.

KRISHNAMURTI : So, how does one get over this barrier? Is it not fairly clear that the word is not the thing? Whether you use an Italian word or an English word or a Greek word, that word is not the thing. The word 'door' is not the door. The word, the description, the explanation, is not the thing explained or described : if this is seen, then there is no longer a dependency on the mere word. Now thought is manufactured of words; thought is always responding, according to memory, in verbal structures. Thought is limited by words, is the slave of words. Can one listen without the word interfering? You say to me 'I love you', but what happens there? The words do not mean anything at all; but there may be a feeling of relationship which has not been brought about by the response of thought to the words; there may be a direct communication. So the mind, being aware that the word is not the thing, that the word, which is thought, interferes, listens freely, without prejudice,—as it does when you say 'I love you'.

Can you listen without interpreting, without your prejudices interfering, twisting—listen as you may listen to the song of a bird? (In Italy there are so few birds; they kill them. What monstrous people we are.) Can you listen to the song of the bird without verbal comment, without naming it, saying, 'It is a blackbird', 'I would like to go on listening to it'; can you listen without any of that interference, just listen—eh? You can, can you not? Now : can you listen equally to what goes on in yourself?—without prejudice, without a formula, without distortion—just as you may listen to that bell (*noise of bell*) without any association, just listening to the pure sound of it; then you are the sound, you are not listening to the sound as something separate.

Questioner: To do this we need to practise.

KRISHNAMURTI : To so listen you need to practise! Somebody
must teach you! The moment somebody teaches you, you
have the guru and the disciple, the authority and the learner.
Now when that bell rang, did you listen to it—without any
interpretation, with complete attention? If you saw that you
said to yourself, 'It is mid-day', 'What time is it?', 'It is meal
time', then you saw that you were not actually giving complete attention to that sound; so you learnt—you were not
taught—that you were not listening.

*Questioner: There is a difference between a bell ringing or a
bird singing, on the one hand, and a word in a sentence which
is interlaced with other words. I can isolate the sound of a
bird, but a word in a sentence I cannot isolate.*

KRISHNAMURTI : Listening to a bird is objective, outside. But
can I listen to myself using a word in the context of a sentence; can I listen to the word and be free of the word and
its context?
    You may say: 'That is a beautiful table.' You have given
that table certain appreciation; you have called it beautiful.
I may look at it and say: 'What an ugly table.' So the word
denotes your feeling; it is not the actual thing; it comes into
being as an associated idea. Can you look at your friend without the image you have created about that friend—the image
being the word, the symbol? We cannot, because we do not
know how that image has been built. You tell me something,
which is pleasurable, and I create an image out of that, that
you are my friend; another tells me something which is unpleasant, similarly I build an image; when I meet you it is
as a friend, when I meet another it is not as a friend. But can
the mind not build an image at all, though you say pleasant or
unpleasant things? It *can* stop building the image when I

give attention; then there is no image-formation; I can listen
—listen without any image.

*Questioner: Would it be possible to go back to what you were
saying at the beginning, about changing ourselves in society?
How is it possible to really change yourself when you are
obliged to conserve your relationships. I am in the Capitalist
world and all my relations have to be capitalistic otherwise I
would starve.*

KRISHNAMURTI: And if you lived in the Communist world,
you would also adjust yourself there.

Questioner: Exactly.

KRISHNAMURTI: So what will you do?

Questioner: How can I change?

KRISHNAMURTI: You have put the question: if I live in a
capitalist society I have to adjust myself to the capitalist demands; yet if I lived in a Communist society, totalitarian,
bureaucratic society, I would also have to do exactly the same
things—so what will I do?

Questioner: I do not think it would be the same thing.

KRISHNAMURTI: But it is the same pattern. There you might
have short hair and you would have to go to work, do this
or that. But it is within the same whirlpool. What will you
do? A human being, realising that change within himself is
of primary importance—whether he lives here or there—

where is his concern? He must change himself: what does
this change imply? Freedom from psychological fear, freedom from greed, envy, jealousy, dependency; freedom from
the fear of being lonely, from the fear of conformity—right?
If you have all these things working inside you—realising no
conformity—you live as well as you can, there or here. But,
unfortunately for us, the important thing is not revolution
inwardly but changing this and that externally.

Questioner: And then what happens if someone kills you?

KRISHNAMURTI: Ah! No one can kill a free man. They can
put his eyes out; inwardly he is free, nothing can touch that
freedom.

Questioner: Would you give a definition of egoism?

KRISHNAMURTI: If you want a definition look it up in a dictionary. 'Definition'—please, I have said very carefully that
the description is not the described. What is this self that is
isolating itself all the time? Even though you love somebody,
whether you sleep with that somebody, etc., there is always
this self which is separate—with its ambitions, its fears, its
agonies, with its occupation with itself in self-pity. As long as
that self exists there must be separation, as long as that exists
there must be conflict—right? How is that self to disappear—
without effort? The moment you make an effort, there is the
'Higher Self', so-called, that is dominating the 'lower self.'
How can the mind dissipate this thing called 'the self'? What
is the self?—is it a bundle of memories?—or is it something
permanent? If it is a bundle of memories, it is of the past; that
is the only thing you have, it is nothing permanent. The self
is the 'me' that has accumulated knowledge and experience,

as memory, as pain; and that becomes the centre from which all action takes place. See it actually as it is.

Every religion, every society and culture, realises that 'the self' wants to express itself; in art, self-expression is tremendously important; it is also very important in its assertion to dominate. Every religion has tried to destroy the self—'Do not bother about the self,' 'Put God in its place, or the State in its place'. And that has not succeeded. The self has identified itself with God—whatever that is—and so it remains. We are saying : observe that self in operation, learn about it, watch it, be aware of it, do not destroy it, do not say, 'I must get rid of it' or 'must change it', just watch it, without any choice, without any distortion; then *out of that watching and learning, the self disappears.*

Rome. 21 October 1970.

73 74 75   12 11 10 9 8 7 6 5 4 3 2